I0140745

The Times of the Judges:
Occupying the Land

A simplified history
of the area of Palestine
during the
times when Judges
ruled Israel

This is the third book in a trilogy
that also includes
two books of historical fiction:
Judges, Rulers and One Angry Levite
and *Samuel, Seer.*

Gordon C. Krantz

This book and the other two books
of the trilogy are
available at
gnrkrantz@aol.com
(recommended)
or
952-881-0449

They are also available from Lulu.com

Copyright © 2008, 2010
Gordon C. Krantz

ISBN 978-0-615-26272-7

I am indebted to the several friends
who have reviewed this book
and recommended changes.
Especially, I wish to thank
Dr. Donald Madvig,
who reviewed it extensively.
Any remaining errors
are the author's sole responsibility.

TABLE OF CONTENTS

Chapter   **Page**

FIGURES

Introduction

This is a book written for the reader who is not an historian but who has read the Bible and is curious about what went on "back then," and who wants to have a better understanding of the actions of the people mentioned in the Books of Judges and First Samuel.

If you are not familiar with the Bible, particularly with the Books of Joshua, Judges, and First Samuel, now would be a good time to at least scan them, because this book is about the times when those events took place. I will mention the characters, of course, but I will not repeat the full stories given in the Bible.

We are used to thinking about the Times of the Judges in the Old Testament as some vague time "back then." We don't think that much else was happening that would have much to do with those separate little stories about people with funny names who did heroic deeds against enemies with even funnier names or who are simply said to have "judged." But all this was part of a bigger picture. There was a lot going on in that part of the world.

The "Times of the Judges" is taken, for our purposes, to be approximately from 1250 BC to 1000 BC. It actually began after the death of Joshua (which must have occurred at some time after 1230 BC, the date of the destruction of Hazor, because Joshua was alive then). The Times of the Judges ended at the death of Samuel, the last Judge. But we will include some time before Joshua died and some time after Samuel died. So this book will cover the times from about 3250 years ago to about 3000 years ago.

To help to visualize that time span we can walk backwards in time, using people who lived *near* each stage for our landmarks, as shown in the table which follows.

Table 1
Timeline

2000+ AD	Our own time; you are here
1500 AD	Christopher Columbus
1000 AD	Lief Erickson, William the Conqueror
500 AD	King Arthur, fall of the Roman Empire
1 AD/1 BC	Jesus Christ
500 BC	Socrates, Esther
1000 BC	King David
1250 – 1000 BC	**The Times of the Judges**
1500 BC	Moses
2000 BC	Abraham

So all the Times of the Judges took place more than 1000 years before the time on earth of Jesus Christ. Those Times ended 3000 years ago. There is good agreement among historians about that ending date. We cannot settle the arguments about the date of the Exodus, so I have chosen what the majority of historians consider to be the approximate date, 1250 BC. If the Times of the Judges began earlier, say 1446 BC as some claim, the difference is only that some events like the battle between Rameses II and the Hittites at Kadesh took place while the Judges carried out their duties; the effect of the great empires on the ground of Canaan was pretty much the same during all that time. Until the middle of the Times, and we'll get to that later.

After the Exodus from Egypt the Israelites entered the Land that they would claim as Abraham's inheritance and began to root out the various peoples who lived there, peoples who are usually called "the Canaanites."

Can we know much about what was going on then, things that would influence the events that we read about in the Books of Judges and First Samuel in our Bible and that

2

might provide more details about them? Actually, we know quite a bit about them both from written sources in addition to the Bible that have been preserved and from the results of modern archaeology. I have not found modern books that focus on that particular time and place.

The major theme of the Times of the Judges is plain in the Book itself. The main theme of the Book of Judges is a repeating cycle of religious decay, followed by oppression by enemies, followed by deliverance under a "judge," followed by reform (usually), followed by religious decay again, and so on. However, there are also stories in the Books that stand in their own right, not related to the major theme.

The Israelites had been given the Law under Moses but they began to fall away from it under the influence of the religions of the native Canaanites. Then, as predicted, outsiders would come in and oppress Israel until the providence of the LORD or some spark of repentance brought forth a deliverer. And that deliverer would be called a Judge.

(Right away you have discovered my attitude about the Books of Joshua, Judges and First Samuel, where the Bible records the Times of the Judges. The Books are taken as the best source of information that we have about the Judges and about Israel of that time. Some people reject any historic validity of the Bible out of hand. Some maintain that its original sources could not have been written near the time of the events. For a number of reasons I believe that Samuel wrote down the root source of the Book of Judges. It may have been edited later, but Samuel was certainly capable of writing it and the socio-religious circumstances of early Israel were certainly capable of preserving it. There are those who maintain that the Books of Joshua and Judges were either first written or completely changed about the time of David or during the return from the Babylonian exile. However, those claims have really little to go for them except a supposition that they were true and the fact that it was possible. No one makes any such argument about other ancient texts that have much poorer preservation and attestation than the Book of Judges. The Books of Joshua, Judges and First Samuel remain the best *written* source we have for the history of that period within the Land of Israel.)

The process of taking over the Land took some time, and it wasn't completed until after David took the throne in about the year 1000 BC. The Book of Joshua in the Bible recounts some of the early take-over action, but of course it only it reports only some of the actions and locations. Meanwhile, there were momentous events and people which impacted the process of occupation and which are not mentioned in the Bible because they were just not part of the central story that make up the message of the Books of Joshua and Judges and the purpose for which they were written.

To understand the setting of the Book of Judges we will here first describe the world in which the Israelite occupation of Canaan took place. Then we will move on to examine the events and people who impacted both the occupation of the Land and the activities of the Judges, including of Samuel. Lastly this book will describe the situation with which the Book of Judges closes and the more settled situation that came about soon afterward. Maps will be provided to help with understanding the context in which the judges acted.

This is not a "historian's book." No serious historian or student of history will find anything new, and will probably find that my choice of the available theories and viewpoints can be argued against. On the other hand, every reasonable attempt has been made to reconcile the conflicting theories and the disputed details that plague that long-ago time in which the non-Biblical sources of information are often fragmentary or hard to interpret. Note that most arguments are about exact dates and origins of peoples, not about the essence of the events. This is not the place for a critical review of all the disputes. This book is written for the more casual reader who only wants to get a grasp of what was going on, the events and circumstances that color and tie together the stories in the Books of Judges and First Samuel.

You are encouraged to read the Books of Joshua and Judges and First Samuel for yourself. For those who wish to pursue a more thorough study of this period in time, a short list of helpful readings is given in Appendix A at the end of this book. It is a short list, but the person who becomes interested in a broader understanding will find more leads as he or she pursues these.

For those who don't want to "study history" but who want to get a sense of the world of the Judges, I recommend my two previous books, *Judges, Rulers and One Angry Levite* and *Samuel, Seer*. Those books are historical fictions that attempt to give the information by means of stories, footnoted as necessary. They can stand alone, and this book is one extended footnote to them.

Just Before the Times of the Judges

The date of 1300 BC, *50 years before* the Times of the Judges, provides a convenient place to start an understanding of the times. The map of Figure 1 gives a wide view of the world of 1300 BC. The view is wider than you will find in most Bibles because, while the area we are examining most closely is only the eastern end of the Mediterranean Sea, the rest of the world also mattered.

This date of 1300 BC was chosen because it explains the Land, the forces that enabled and hindered Israel, the regional international situation in which Joshua led Israel into Canaan and in which the Israelite's occupation began, and the world in which the Judges acted.

The first thing to understand about the world of that time is that there were no national boundaries. Throughout most of Europe, northern Africa, and western Asia most people were nomads, farmers, herders, or hunter-gatherers, without any awareness of belonging to a nation. They were simply the people who lived in a particular area and who usually spoke the same language. If they felt that they "belonged to" something, it was usually to a clan or a village or maybe a city or to a chieftain or small king of some kind. And if they lived inside one of the few areas controlled by an empire, well, the Emperor was far away.

There were political entities of sorts, most of them being a city with a leader who thought of himself as a king and who in some sense ruled the surrounding countryside. And there were two great empires, each of which controlled the political entities in their spheres of influence.

The part of the world that we are considering in most of this book is the Levant. A word about terminology is in order here. I chose "the Levant" instead of either the

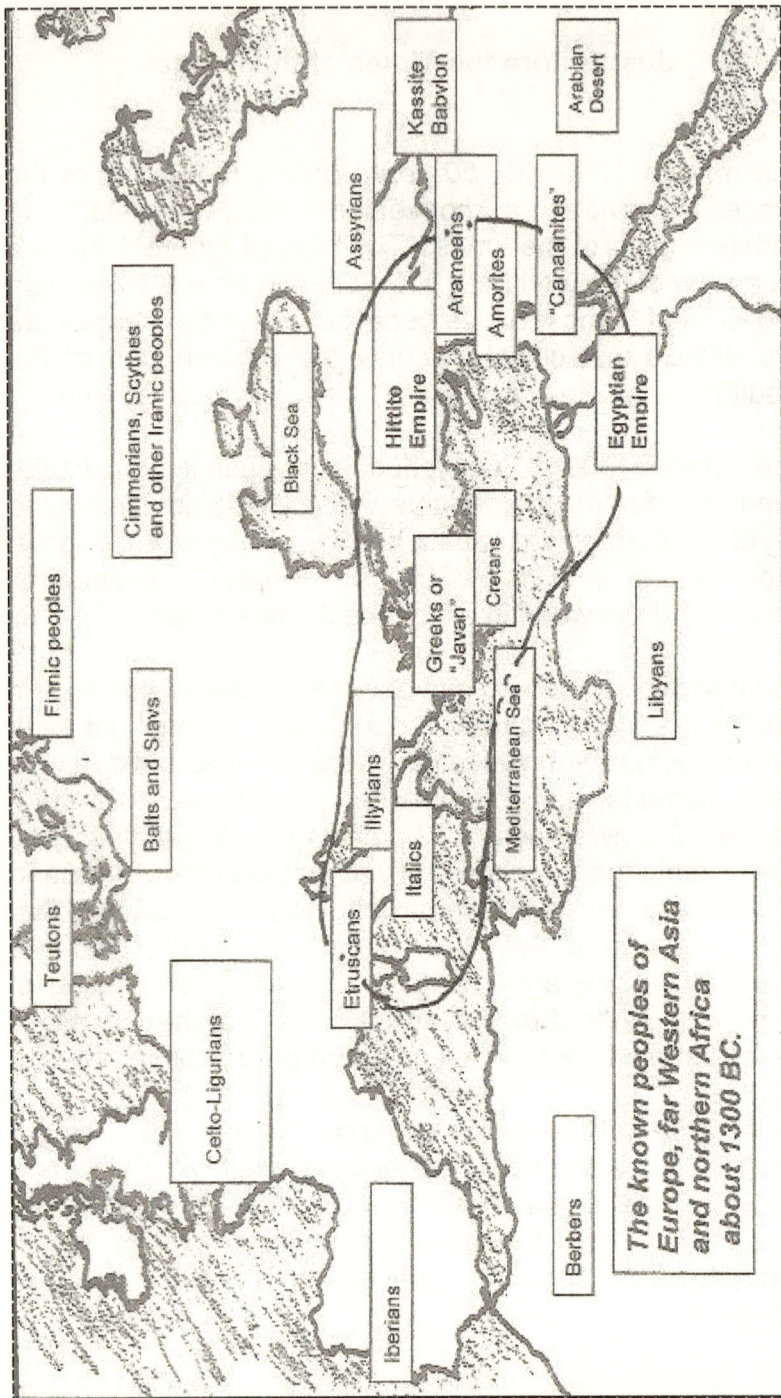

The known peoples of Europe, far Western Asia and northern Africa about 1300 BC.

Labels on map:
Kassite Babylon
Arabian Desert
Assyrians
Arameans
Amorites
"Canaanites"
Egyptian Empire
Hittite Empire
Cimmerians, Scythes and other Iranic peoples
Black Sea
Finnic peoples
Balts and Slavs
Greeks or "Javan"
Cretans
Mediterranean Sea
Illyrians
Italics
Libyans
Teutons
Etruscans
Celto-Ligurians
Iberians
Berbers

Middle East or the Near East, because those terms cover too wide an area. The Levant has variable definitions, but here it refers to the eastern part of the Mediterranean region. It includes modern Egypt, Palestine, Syria, Lebanon, and at least the eastern half of Turkey. Inland to the east, it ranges as far as the modern capitol of Jordan, Amman, and it includes the Sinai Peninsula. To its northeast it includes the headwaters of the great rivers Tigris and Euphrates, but it does not include those rivers' lower regions, which we call Mesopotamia. Figure 2 shows this definition of the Levant.

I will also refer to "the Land," by which is meant the land that was promised to Abraham and which we think of as Canaan proper after it was allotted to the tribes of Israel.

Even the two great empires in the Levant, those of the Hittites (Hittites are the people, and Hatti is the nation) and of the Egyptians, did not have boundaries. The empires ended at the edges where the central power and control faded away at some practical distance from the center, with such natural barriers as rivers or mountains only rarely determining the accepted or contested borders. The border of the third great empire, the Chinese Shang Empire with still 200 years to run, was too far away to affect our story.

Peoples. There were people all over except in deep deserts, though they might be widely scattered. Fragmentary preserved records, archaeology and languages give us information about where these peoples lived. The map in Figure 1 shows some of them. A line on the map is drawn around the peoples who would impact the Israelites as they struggled through the Times of the Judges. Notice how far westward was the origin of some of those peoples.

Let us take a quick look at the peoples of the wider world. We can identify them from archaeology and sometimes from history. First, the peoples who are *not* inside the line

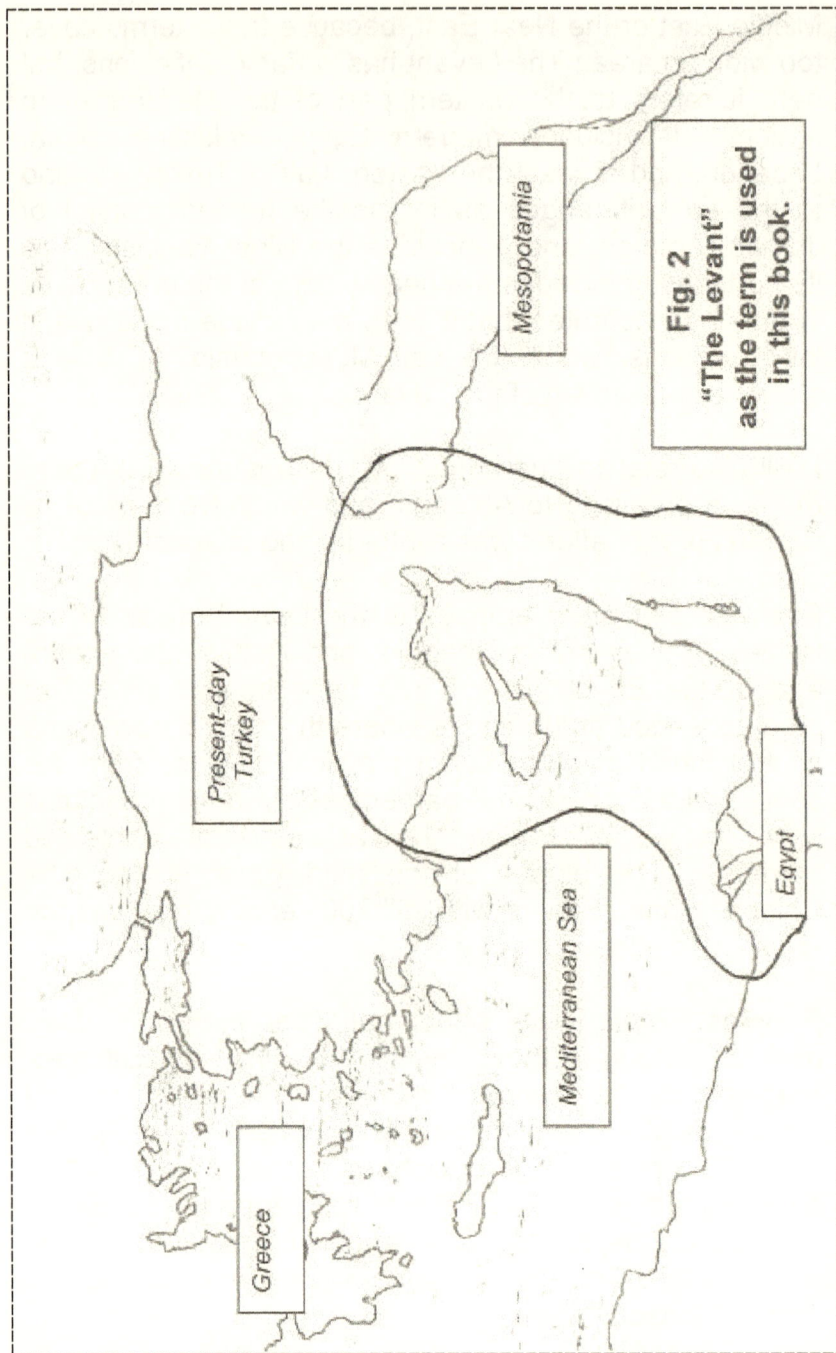

Fig. 2
"The Levant"
as the term is used
in this book.

drawn on the map of Fig. 1, and who did *not* impact the Land directly at that time, but who might be interesting to us. Among them were the ancestors of most of us.

The Finnic peoples were the ancestors (at least linguistically) of the present Finns, Estonians, Saami (Lap), and Hungarians, and probably of the Turkic peoples. The many Finnic peoples occupied much of Russia and all of present-day Finland, but also some of northern and eastern Europe, except for the southern end of the Scandinavian Peninsula.

The Teutons who lived south of them on the Scandinavian Peninsula and into Denmark were the ancestors of the modern Scandinavians, Germans, Dutch, Frisians, Goths and the people who much later invaded England as the Anglo-Saxons.

The Balts are now represented by the Latvians and Lithuanians. The Prussians, who were also Balts and not Germans, have been absorbed into the peoples of Poland and Latvia.

The Slavs, after much wandering, gave rise to the Russians, Poles, Czechs, Yugoslavs, and their relatives.

The Celto-Ligurians were the ancestors of at least the Celtic peoples, now represented by the Irish, the Scots, and the Bretons of far-west France. They contributed to the old genetic stock of other parts of Europe, especially of France.

The Illyrians were the probable ancestors of the modern Albanians.

The Berbers represent the Cushites, who were broadly distributed in Africa. In North Africa, they

11

were the ancestors and relatives of the Berbers, Moroccans and Libyans. Other Cushites lived in the dry lands of northern Africa, even to the south of Egypt and the Horn of Africa.

The Assyrians at that time, who were Semites like their neighbors to the south, were not yet an empire and were at this time a small buffer state between the Hittites and the Babylonians. Their impact on Israel during the Times of the Judges was only indirect.

The Kassites who ruled Babylonia are not well defined; they seem to have been Indo-European. They had ruled over a population of Babylonians for perhaps 200 years.

All these peoples, who were important to themselves and who may be your ancestors, were outside the region which impacted Israel and the Land, and they have been left outside of the line drawn on the map in Figure 1.

Now consider the peoples who are *inside* the line drawn on the map. They are the peoples who did make an impact upon the Israelites as they occupied the Land.

We will later describe the Hittites and the Egptians.

The Canaanites, the Amorites and the Aramaeans made major impacts on Israel. Some historians count all the Canaanites, Amorites, Amalekites and similar peoples as subdivisions of the Aramaeans. They, like the Israelites, were Semites, as were the Midianites who seem to have come from the Arabian Desert and to have been related to the modern Arabs. (You will find fuller definitions of these and other peoples in Appendix B.)

The Greeks of that day were the Mycenaean Greeks of Homer and the Trojan War and were part of the mix that makes up modern Greece. A sophisticated Cretan civilization flourished on the island of Crete, independently at first, but by 1300 BC they were under the rule of the Mycenaean Greeks. There is a strong relationship between these peoples and the later Philistines.

In Italy, the Etruscans were then stronger than the Italics; they disappeared as a language group, but of course their genes live on in northern Italy. The Italics became ancestors of the Romans and others. These peoples and others from as far west as Sicily would later make a major impact on the Land as components of the Sea Peoples.

Many of the peoples who existed then, such as the Iberians, faded from history as identifiable groups. Some of their genes are preserved in those who absorbed or conquered them. For that matter, all modern groups are the result of mergers and submergences; we are all of mixed ancestry and nobody is "pure" anything. The possible exception is the Cohen or priestly line of Jews, whose Y-chromosomes appear to be lineal, but even they cannot vouch for their maternal lines via DNA.

The peoples who mattered most to the world at that time were those of the Egyptian and Hittite Empires. They were the Great Powers of their day. They were the forces that were most instrumental in setting the stage for the Israelite conquest of Canaan and for the Times of the Judges. Let us look at them. It will be helpful to start just before the Times of the Judges, in 1300 BC, as shown in the map of Figure 3.

Egypt. Egypt was old. Its pyramids had already been old by the time of Abraham. Like all old cultures, by the time we are discussing it had roots that were fossilized in ritual and formula, so old that some of the meaning of the formulas had been forgotten. Egypt's religion was polytheistic, with many animal-headed gods who probably

13

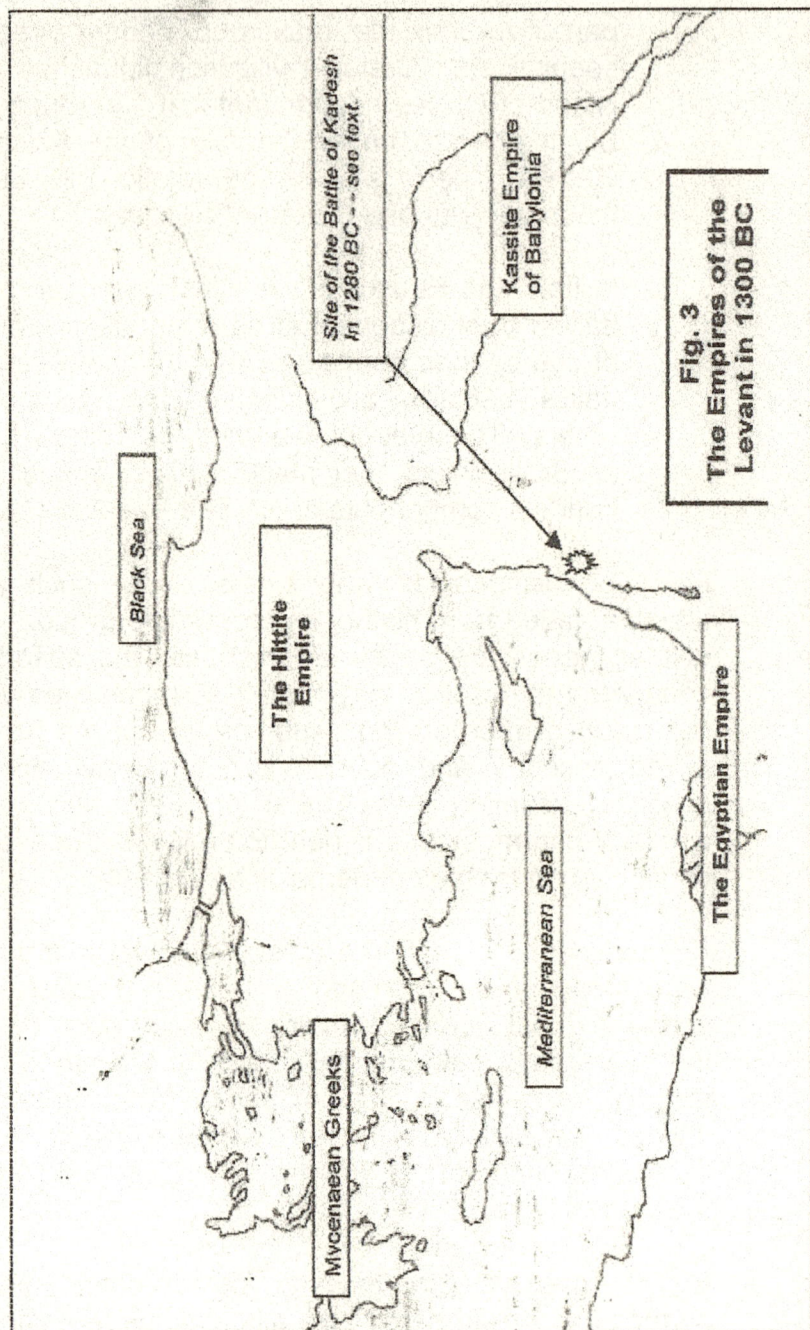

Black Sea

The Hittite Empire

Mycenaean Greeks

Mediterranean Sea

The Egyptian Empire

Site of the Battle of Kadesh in 1280 BC -- see text.

Kassite Empire of Babylonia

Fig. 3
The Empires of the
Levant in 1300 BC

began as totems of various cities and regions. The mythology was pretty basic. For example, the creation myth did involve particular gods, but the other relationships among the gods were variable. Some were thought to be related to each other, many were not.

Pharaoh was a god. He was not the incarnation of any of the other gods, but he was a god in his own right, just because he was Pharaoh (the name is a title, meaning "Great House" -- like our White House). Although he might refer to one of the gods as his father, he might so refer to more than one god. Rameses II, in boasting of his valor in a battle, claimed to be "like my father Month," a war god. In the same battle he claimed Amon as his father, and also that "this [Rameses] was Sutekh, Baal was in his limbs."

Egypt was resistant to change. A century before the Times of the Judges, Egypt had undergone a failed religious revolution. The Pharaoh Akhenaten conceived of a sole god, personified as the sun. He wrote hymns to the god, the Aten, hymns that resemble our Book of Psalms. This resemblance is not surprising, because cultures tend to have regional similarities, and there are deeply shared, almost universal, ways of expressing religious ecstasy and adoration. Akhenaten tried to impose his vision onto the whole nation and he nearly succeeded. However, the Aten religion did not survive him, and by the Times of the Judges Egypt was back to its age-old religious routines where the chief god was Amun. Akhenaten's son, Tut-ankh-aten, changed his name to Tut-ankh-amen (King Tut to us). Akhenaten was not a good executive. If he had been successful in his religious reform to monotheism, history might have been different.

The common people of Egypt were peasants and craftsmen and they were technically servants or slaves of Pharaoh. They would have said that they had good lives. There was usually enough to eat and the food was varied with grain and vegetables and fruits and occasional meat

15

or fish. Their skeletons say that there was not enough protein, though. The warm climate made elaborate houses and clothing unnecessary. Being common people in a low-literacy age, they left no monuments or diaries, although archaeologists have excavated their villages and from that we know something about how they lived. We have no record of whether they believed in an after-life for themselves. They must have really believed in the divinity of Pharaoh because they seem to have never revolted. Enslaved foreigners like the Children of Israel might revolt, but not the Egyptian peasant farmers. The Nile might not rise enough to flood and fertilize the fields and famine might result, but hey, things happen. As in every pre-industrial age, peasants made up the durable base of civilization.

For centuries Egypt had exercised some control over the southern half of the eastern Mediterranean shore and its ports, as far north as into modern Lebanon and Syria. But before 1300 BC Egypt had drifted into the interesting but ineffective dynasty of Akhenaten and his son Tutankhaten or Tutankhamen. The clay tablets found in their old foreign office archives reflect the distress of the coastal cities in Syria, which were being overrun by nomads while the Pharaohs ignored them. The dynasty of Akhenaten nearly lost the Egyptian empire.

But after that dynasty came Seti I and his son, the great Rameses II. Both of them raided through Palestine and Syria, Seti I as far as northern Lebanon. Yet the ongoing interest of those great pharaohs was pretty much limited to the coastal cities, and they left the inland city-states as they always were, disunited and ignored. Egypt did intervene when one of the cities attacked the Egyptian garrison at Beth Shean. Egypt apparently did not leave standing armies in the central hill country or the Jordan valley, and after each military campaign it withdrew its armies to the delta and valley of the Nile.

16

Then came the famous drive of Rameses II into Syria in 1280 BC to meet the forces of the Hittite Empire.

The Hittites. The Hittites were not an imaginary people, as was thought by many historians until the late 19th Century. The Bible was then the only record that mentioned them and the other ancient historians left no trace of anyone called Hittite. So that part of the Bible was discounted as imaginary. It wasn't until the clay tablets of Akhenaten's foreign office in Egypt were found in 1887 and deciphered that a large body of evidence about the Hittites came to light.

It has since been established by archaeological findings in Turkey and Egypt that the Hittites were indeed an empire and that they occupied what is now western Turkey for some 500 years until about 1178 BC. Their writings show that they were Indo-European, and furthermore that they were the first of our linguistic group to develop writing, centuries before the Greeks did. (English is a Teutonic or Germanic language in the Indo-European group. The Indo-European languages include Hittite, Germanic, Italic, Greek, Slavic, Iranian, Indic, Celtic, etc. Indo-European is totally different from Semitic or Finnic or from Egyptian.)

Well, we know that the ruling classes of the Hittites who left documents in clay and stone were Indo-European. We don't know much about the lower classes, who were probably a native people whom the Hittites had conquered. There is some argument among historians about that. It looks at though the Hittites had invaded what is now central Turkey some time between 2000 BC and 1700 BC. There were people living there already, though we don't know who they were. The scant evidence we have of their language shows it was not like Hittite. The result was the inevitable mix that follows an invasion, tempered by the also inevitable initial segregation of conquerors from the commoners and then the slow breakdown of that segregation. The portraits of Hittite individuals, both their own and the Egyptian's

17

portraits, do not flatter them. They seem to have had unusually big noses and to have dressed in bulgy clothes. And yes, their shoes had turned-up toes.

The religion of the Hittites was polytheistic. The most popular god was Teshub, the storm god. On the other hand, the Hittites seem not to have minded swearing by gods of other nations, such as those of the Babylonians, in their legal documents.

At any rate the Hittite Empire was a Great Power for hundreds of years. At one time it even temporarily conquered Babylon.

Clash, and a treaty. In 1280 BC, some 30 years before the date I have taken as the start of the Times of the Judges, the two Great Powers came to a decisive clash.

Recall that there were no national borders, only spheres of control that faded out at the edges. Northern Palestine and Syria made up one such edge. Egypt controlled the coast north into Syria and had nominal control over the hinterland. The Hittites had spread into northern Syria. Rameses II was full of himself and was not yet the old, wily Pharaoh that he would later become in his 92 years. He seems to have decided to make good his claim to the northern half of the east Mediterranean coast.

Both of the great empires were at their peaks. The Hittites had shown their power in Mesopotamia and the whole north. Egypt was riding the tides of Seti I and Rameses II. The border between the empires was undefined and both had thrust into it. This was for all the marbles. There were some 20,000 troops on each side, the largest armies that the Middle East had known to that date.

Rameses personally led four corps of troops, heavily invested in chariots, north to take on the Hittites. King Muwatallis of Hatti led his army south with at least as many chariots to meet him. They encountered each other at Kadesh, a city on the Orontes River in Syria, in the valley we now call the Bekaa Valley and which is best known in modern times as the headquarters of Hezbollah. The site of the ensuing battle is marked with a star in Figure 3. The two empires had scribes whose records have been preserved in enough detail for us to learn just how the battle went. Rameses had been rash. He rode into an ambush, and only escaped by personal valiant effort and good fortune. The battle was a sort of draw, but in actuality it was close to a Hittite victory. Muwatallis went home satisfied and Rameses went home pretending that he had won and that the army of Hittites had been destroyed. The scribes of both empires described the battle in terms flattering to their rulers. The real outcome was that Rameses had to give up his northern push.

But the outcome that matters most to us, and that establishes the Battle of Kadesh as one of the most decisive battles of the ancient world, is that about 11 years later, in 1269 BC, Rameses made a peace treaty with the next Hittite king, Hattusilis. To seal the treaty Rameses took to wife a daughter of Hattusilis and made her his chief wife. The treaty was inscribed on a silver plaque (now lost, of course) of which copies in clay and in stone have been found in Turkey and in Egypt. The treaty settles details about military limits, trade, and deserters or refugees. The treaty lasted 70 years – the longest peace that that large area of the Middle East has known.

Other peoples and empires. The map in Figure 3 shows two other significant "empires." In Babylon, the Kassites had taken over rulership and territory. Their line of kings would last another 200 years, though their interests did not extend far enough west to have any real effect on the Land we are discussing. The Mycenaean Greeks were not an empire, though culturally they almost amounted to one. They were chieftain-ruled cities and territories, often at odds with each other but still unified enough to be seen by their neighbors as one people. They ruled the large

19

and civilized island of Crete as well as the mainland and the islands along the coast of what is now Turkey. The main event for which we now know them, the Trojan War, was still 200 years in the future. The Israelites, insofar as they knew of the Greeks, called them "the Javan," or as we would say, the Ionians.

Canaan did not count as an empire. Each city-state was an entity to its own. We aren't even certain that the peoples of that day even thought of the Canaanites as one people. The Egyptians may have thought of them as "Asians." Various Canaanite cities are mentioned in the fragmentary preserved records of contemporary peoples, but always individually rather than as part of a nation.

Actually, while we tend to call of the peoples in the Land Canaanites, the Canaanites predominated in the foothills and plains toward the Mediterranean Sea and in the Jordan valley, while the hill country between was mostly Amorite. We will usually call them all Canaanites in this book.

The Land prepared. It was in the middle of that 70-year treaty between the Hittites and Egypt that I think Joshua entered into the Land and began the occupation of Canaan. Curiously, few historians take note of that signally important fact. Could this be the reference behind the statement (Numbers 14:9) that "their (the Canaanites' and the Amorites') protection is gone," with "gone" implying that the protection of Egypt was once there, but is no more? At any rate, the peace treaty between Egypt and Hatti (the country of the Hittites) would have provided an opportunity to Joshua.

What was the socio-political situation he found? First, the Land was officially demilitarized. Rameses had withdrawn his army, and the treaty specified that neither he nor the Hittites would mount military occupation in that buffer zone. Egypt retained nominal control of Canaan, but in the absence of an occupying army it was not effective.

Further, Egypt did not much care about anything but the coastal cities, because those cities could get for them the resources of the hinterland, such as Lebanese timber.

Second, this left Canaan in the control of many separate city-states, and they were not united. The king of Megiddo might levy toll at the crossroads of the two main commercial routes that his fortress overlooked, but what happened to the city-state of Hazor was not his concern. The king of Beth Shean had his fort and its valley, and he had no concern for the king of little Bethel or Ai or Shiloh. The king of Jericho 'way down in the Jordan Valley was of no concern to the King of Salem or Jebus (now known as Jerusalem) - - although after Jericho fell, King Adnoi Salem (translated as "the Lord of Salem") became alarmed enough to assemble a coalition to fight Joshua.

So the army of an empire would not confront Israel, only the troops and walls of small city-states.

Then, about 1277 BC, after the battle of Kadesh and before the time that I think Israel entered Canaan, Rameses had another military engagement that foreshadowed what was coming later. He fought a successful sea battle with a people called the Sherdan and incorporated the surrendered men into his own army. The Sherdan he fought were the vanguard of a host of mixed people, including other Sherdan, who would loom large in the history of Israel. That host was the Sea Peoples, whom I will discuss in a later chapter. At the time, Rameses' victory was a mere footnote to his career. It is only now that we can see it as the model for the later invasion: a mass movement of a new people into the Middle East, and the incorporation of the defeated or stalemated fighting men into the Egyptian army.

And the Children of Israel were still slaving away in northeast Egypt, making brick for Rameses' great construction projects in the royal city of Pi-Rameses.

The Canaan
that Israel Walked into

If we take the beginning of the Times of the Judges to be about 1250 BC, then the great empires were still in place. Thanks to their peace treaty, they did not have armies in Canaan, though there were probably some Egyptian garrisons in major cities. Egypt was not strongly engaged, at any rate.

The world empires. Egypt was still great but was now less inclined to take more than an episodic interest in Canaan. It was enough to make a periodic swing through, mostly in the coastal area, with an army of greater or lesser size. Pharaoh Merneptah made a raid through to Syria about 1225 BC and boasted (among other triumphs) that Israel "is no more;" this could mean anything from the destruction of some Israelite settlements to exacting a pledge from some leader to remain faithful to the Egyptian overlordship. Merneptah's "destruction" of Israel is not recorded in the Books of Joshua or Judges. With the Rameses-Hattusilis treaty still in nominal effect, Merneptah could hardly keep his army in Canaan. But the report of his raid is important to us because it does prove that the Israelites were in Canaan in 1225 BC, some 25 years after their entry under Joshua.

The Hittite empire was not exactly in decline but it was not pushing its southern border either. Its greatness at that time was of a different kind. The king, Hatusilis III, has left us what is considered the first true autobiography of a ruler, and he displayed a remarkable understanding of his effect on history and of the justification and consequences of his acts. His autobiography shows a humility that is the exact opposite of the grandiosity of Rameses the Great. We Indo-Europeans had our first literature. Other civilizations (Egypt, Babylonia, maybe Harappa in what is now Pakistan, and the northwest Semites) had been writing for centuries. It would be a long time before the other Indo-Europeans, the Greeks, would have a written as opposed to a chanted literature. Nevertheless, the end of the Hittite Empire was approaching.

Egypt respected the north-Syrian demarcation line between the empires. The Hittites from this time on made no more moves toward the south. Neither empire interfered with the Israelite conquest of Canaan. And a few decades later, the Hittite empire was destroyed and disappeared from history until it was dug up less than 150 years ago.

Canaan. The country of Canaan, like other areas, did not have a political boundary when Joshua led the Israelites into it. So we don't have a map with a boundary to represent "this is what everyone at the time thought of as Canaan." We make do with the territories that were assigned to the Tribes of Israel, and we call that territory "Canaan." The closely related or even identical people who lived outside the Israelite tribal allotments, such as the residents of Sidon who were later called Phoenicians, could not have been differentiated at the time from other Canaanites, but we don't say that they lived in Canaan because their territory had not been allotted to an Israelite tribe. Remember, there were no political entities with marked boundaries. So when we identify Canaan with the tribal allotments of Israel, we're being arbitrary.

I am not aware of any explicit statement of national boundaries that has come down to us from earlier than this time. The description of Joshua's tribal allotments in Canaan seems to be unique.

This Canaan was bounded on the west by the Mediterranean Sea. On the south the border was officially the River of Egypt, a dry wadi south of the modern Gaza Strip. This southern border looped southeast, then northeast, to the southern end of the Dead Sea.

The eastern border began midway on the Dead Sea at the Arnon River, swung out eastward to just west of the modern Jordanian capitol of Amman, then it continued northward in a broad loop to just south of Damascus. You notice that this eastern border takes in a large area east of the Jordan, in what is now the nation called Jordan. The residents of that area were not exactly what we would otherwise call Canaanites, and it was not part of the territiory that was allotted by Moses to the tribes of Israel. It was, however, a territory that was allotted to 2-1/2 tribes by Joshua. Many modern Bibles display fine maps of the tribal allotments. These maps should be consulted.

From north of Damascus, the northern border looped over to the Mediterranean Sea just north of Tyre. The western border of the land was, of course, the Mediterranean Sea.

There are two exceptions to that description of the boundaries of Canaan. First, Israel did not successfully take the land along the Mediterranean coast south of Tyre (a city which David did not take) until King David decisively defeated the Philistines after the Times of the Judges. Second, the Bible gives two descriptions of the eastern boundary of the Land of Israel. Above, I traced borders that include the land east of the Jordan River, the part occupied by the Israelite tribes of Reuben, Gad, and half the tribe of Manasseh. Yet in Numbers 34, the LORD commanded Moses to tell Israel that its eastern border from the Sea of Galilee to the Dead Sea was to be the Jordan River, though the area east of the Jordan was actually taken over by Israel.

So there are two definitions of Canaan, one which includes land east of the Jordan and one which does not. In this book, we will continue to treat the part east of the Jordan River as part of Canaan, although it was geographically and culturally a bit different. .

In those days Canaan was physically quite different from what we see today. Now the very lower end of the Jordan

25

valley is desolate, like the South Dakota Badlands. Then it was lush and even jungley, where foreign rulers had hunted elephants and hippos, not to mention the Asian lions and the bears that were found elsewhere in Canaan. The foothills west of the Jordan were fertile, and there were many towns that served the trade route from Arabia that crossed the Jordan and passed by Megiddo to the seacoast south of Tyre.

The Mediterranean coastal plain was also well watered, and it housed large towns. These included the cities of Gath and Ashdod and Gaza, which at that time were not yet Philistine cities because the Philistines had not yet arrived. There had been hippos and crocodiles in the streams that entered the Mediterranean and the streams were larger in those days.

A few locations between the Jordan Valley and the Sea supported large towns where springs brought water to them. Jericho had a huge spring, and Salem (modern Jerusalem) had the Gihon Spring. Farther to the north was Megiddo, with a spring and a site overlooking and controlling the intersection of the two main trade routes. With the exception of the hill country, Canaan was well populated.

The hill country in those days was also quite different from what it is now. Then, it was forested. It wasn't unpopulated, but it was populated much more sparsely than the rest of the country. Not incidentally it is in this sparsely populated hill country that modern archaeologists find the earliest evidence of Israelite occupation.

The least-populated parts of Canaan were the southern deserts, now called the Negev. Even there, though, there were groves of trees. The Negev south of modern Jerusalem was dry country even in Joshua's time. The land could support flocks of sheep and goats but not extensive crop agriculture. It grew grain less easily than did the better-watered areas to the north, though in those days it grew grain better than it does now.

To the limited extent that Canaan had any political entities, those entities were city-states. "The king" was the title of the leader of a city. His "kingdom" extended as far as his power and influence would reach, and that was variable. He might or might not have a number of surrounding villages which owed him allegiance and received protection in times of trouble, and which looked to him as a leader. Many cities had walls because there was occasional inter-city strife. There was no pretense, usually, that these walls were strong enough to hold against an Egyptian army, only against nomadic raiders.

Along the coastal plain Egypt was acknowledged as some sort of supreme power. But inland in the hill country, and especially 'way down in the Jordan Valley, Egypt was far away.

Canaanites. The Land that the Israelites entered and began to occupy was a land already occupied and with a distinctive culture. For the Twelve Tribes of Israel to claim their allotments they had to displace or overwhelm the current occupants. You should read the Book of Joshua to see the fragmentary record of this process. Other information about the process of occupation is found in the stories of the Judges. The occupation was to be a drawn-out one, with movement forward and back, but a relentless one that culminated in the kingdom established under King David. It was not only an occupation of the Land but also a crisis of identity for both sides.

Canaan had a common basic language, perhaps used in various dialects among all the "...ites" of the land. It would be akin to the Hebrew of the Israelites. From what little is said about it in the Bible, we can infer that the Israelites had continued to use the Northwest Semitic language that developed into Hebrew even when they were in Egypt. This language would have been the one that Abraham and his family adapted, in Canaan, from the generic Aramaean roots that came from Ur and Haran with the Patriarchs' family. It is likely that Israelites and Canaanites could understand each other. From the scraps of writing we find on things like potsherds, by the later Times of the Judges we cannot tell which writer is Canaanite and which is Israelite. The language is "the lip of Canaan."

It is likely that not all residents of Canaan were of the same stock. The great empires and various tribes of Aramaeans had rolled through and had left their genes. There had to be remnants of even earlier peoples in the mix. There were merchants and mercenaries and settlers from other places. A good example is Ephron the Hittite in Hebron who had sold land to Abraham some 500 years earlier. We are used to thinking of "the Canaanites," but probably they didn't think of themselves as one people. They were self-identified as Hivites, Jebusites, Perizzites, and so on, mostly named after their city-states or their putative ancestors. Their genetic mixture is partly reflected in the names of their tribes, though in the nature of human interaction throughout time each of these tribes was itself a genetic mixture.

The Land has always been a corridor for the movement of peoples. The gene pool should have correspondingly reflected that fact, and it is buttressed by modern genetic studies. The Canaanites are usually thought of as a sub-set of Aramaeans, and this no doubt was the genetic core. The Egyptians thought of them as Asiatics, in contrast to civilized People of the Nile like themselves. The Egyptian tomb painters picture Asiatics or Canaanites as wearing long kilts but no doubt they wore cloaks in the colder seasons.

There were urban Canaanites and rural ones. Even in the cities there were many farmers who lived inside the walls and who tended farms just outside them. The rural Canaanites lived very much like the Israelites would do when they came in, tending flocks and olive trees and grape vines, growing barley and wheat. Compared to the Israelites, who were desert-accustomed nomads when they entered Canaan, the local people were sophisticated and town-oriented. They no doubt considered themselves to be civilized, established and comfortable and to have a successful religion and way of life. The Israelites must have looked like bumpkins to them.

The material culture of the Canaanites -- the physical objects they used, the houses they lived in, the clothes they wore -- was similar to the other cultures of the Middle East in the time we call the Late Bronze Age. Their art was, by Egyptian standards, crude but not necessarily ugly. Their main metal was bronze, though it was expensive and flintstone was used for many things such as the cutting edges of grain sickles. They were not a rich people nor were they impoverished. Their houses were small by our standards and the room or rooms were multipurpose. Houses were made of stone or mud brick with timbers to support a roof of packed clay over reed mats. Waterproof plaster had been invented in the recent past, so their underground cisterns were plastered, and this enabled survival in the seasonally drier areas. The recency of this invention probably helps to explain why the hill country of Canaan was not yet densely settled when the Israelites arrived. Significantly, this plaster enabled the Israelites to settle the drier parts of the Land when they arrived.

Canaanite religion. We don't know many details of the religions of the Canaanites. We know the big facts: they worshipped a set of gods of the kinds that were common in the Middle East, with names we are familiar with: Baal, Asherah, El, Moloch. Some of those names are not exactly names as we think of them.

Baal, for example is simply a word that means "lord" or "master." We don't know if he had any other name, though he probably did at the beginning of his religion.

The name was pronounced in two syllables, "Ba'al;" --
BAH-al," or "Buh-AHL." A Canaanite would not know
whom you meant by "Bail." The mythology around him
was that of a vegetation god who was responsible for the
seasonal death (planting of seed) and resurrection
(growth and harvest) of crops. Some think that his proper
name was, at first and maybe later, Hadad, the storm god
of the northern Levant. It is also possible that a different
personality called Baal was conceived by different city-
states, so that there were various local Baals.

(Present-day Israeli and Palestine farmers who don't have
irrigation are said to practice "Baal farming." That is, they
are dependent on the Lord's vagaries of rain. Because
they are either Palestinian and therefore either Muslims or
Christians, or Israeli who are practicing or secular Jews,
no one accuses them of idolatry, but instead we credit
them with dependence on "the Lord.")

A tougher problem is that of the nature of El. Again, El is
more of a title than a personal name. You have to have
some way in any language to say just "God," and
Canaanite and Hebrew were similar enough so that both
would have the same way to say just "God." The linguistic
root appears in the first chapter of our Bible, in that the
world was created by Elohim. (Elohim is "El-plural,"
somewhat as a king refers to himself as "we.")
Throughout the Bible, there are other uses of El in
compound form: El Shaddai, for example. In Canaanite
mythology, El was the father god, the father of the gods
and of man. There may never have been a proper name
for El. El seems to have been conceived of as too high
to be much involved in daily human affairs. It may be that
he was considered too high and distant to write about
casually and this might account for the fact that we don't
know much about the Canaanite conception of him. He
may or may not have been represented by unhewn stone
pillars, and he certainly was sometimes represented by
the image of a bull.

The Asherah was thought of as the wife of El, and also as having other less clearly known functions. She was represented by a wooden pole or a carved upright figure. She may well be related to the even older pagan idea of a mother goddess, who had been the chief ancient god of the whole Middle East. Because the Canaanites certainly saw her as the consort of El, and because some Israelites certainly fell into a form of Canaanite worship, some historians are convinced that El was the same as the Israelite God YHWH or Yahweh (a Name that we have transformed into "Jehovah"), and that "Yahweh had a wife." They think that this was part of the *original* religion of the Israelites. I think that this is an unfounded assumption on the part of those who by faith reject the faiths of Judaism and Christianity. The matter is simply this: the father god of the Canaanites was thought of as having a wife, and some Israelites fell into following or incorporating the Canaanite religion. Then to avoid rejecting their heritage and to still claim that they were worshipping the LORD, they thought that Yahweh was the same as El. We have substantial archaeological evidence that some Israelites mixed the worship of the LORD with elements of the Canaanite religions.

Later, Dagon enters the story. Dagon was originally a grain god of Mesopotamia, adopted enthusiastically by the Philistines especially. He was imaged as a man with a fish tail. He seems not to have been well integrated into the pantheon of Canaan, and he may have in some manner and at some times substituted for Baal.

Moloch is another Canaanite deity, specifically called a god of the Ammonites. We aren't sure when this god became an object of worship, or even if his worship was ever prominent in south Canaanite practice. Again, the name is written identically to a title, that of "King" and is found in Hebrew (and Canaanite) documents written with the letters "mlk." There were only consonants in the written early Semitic alphabet, so the name could have pronounced with different vowels, or even as "Milcom." At

31

times it appears that Moloch was confused with Baal. Sometimes Moloch is identified with the sun god Shemesh, and in the north even with Teshub the Hittite storm god. In any case, when the name appears, it is usually in connection to the sacrificial offering of first-born infants through fire.

There were other gods. Shamesh or Shemesh was the sun god, Mot was the god of death adopted from Egypt, and there were others in this mixture that changed somewhat with location and time.

Surrounding peoples worshiped these gods and also had their own gods. The Moabites, for example, held to the worship of Chemosh as their chief god for centuries, even into the 800s BC.

Canaanite religion may not have ever been a unified system of belief. It seems to have varied over time and especially over space, in that there were many local variants. One image that recurs is the bull that represents El or Baal. We have conflicting and fanciful reports of what Moloch looked like, but no hard evidence. The Asherah poles were apparently of wood, and have long ago perished. Remains of hilltop shrines have been found, with upright stones that may represent El or Asherah. As to Dagon, there is a Mesopotamian relief showing a priest of Dagon, and his fish costume may be a representation of the god (fish head hat, trailing tail). There are sketches preserved on pottery that are said to represent "Yahweh and his Asherah," and they are not attractive drawings.

A feature of Canaanite religion, and indeed of all the pagan religions of that day, is that there seems to be no hint of an obligation to "love the Baal, thy god" or to love any of the gods. And the love of the gods for the people seems to be missing as well. There is evidence of the impulse to worship and honor the gods, and of fear of the gods, and even of receiving the favor of the gods. But the

Canaanite might well ask, "What has love got to do with it?" There is something basically utilitarian about the Canaanite religion as we know it. You do the rites and you get the rain. The Canaanite had obligation to his gods, but apparently love was not one of them. Definitiely not "love the [god] with all your heart, and with all your might…"

For the purposes of the writers of the Biblical books of Joshua and Judges, the essence of the Canaanite religion was that it was an abomination in the LORD's Law of Moses. The gods of Canaan were represented by forbidden "graven images." Worse, they were the "other gods before (beside) Me" that the Law's Commandments expressly forbade. Finally, the religious rituals involved what the Israelites and we would view as immorality. The fertility of the crops was ensured by the fertility of humans, and so the ritual and public sexual union of people was practiced as a symbolic magic to influence the grain, olive and grape harvests. Temple prostitutes played a part in this.

In contrast to its stories of conquered cities, the Bible is almost silent about the day-to-day interactions of invading Israelite individuals with the native Canaanites. At first, the interactions were the simple brutality of conquest. Later, because the Canaanites were conquered but not exterminated (except for a few cities), there had to be those daily interactions. All the Bible gives us is the occasional recorded contact and a great deal of implication about the ways in which Israelites adapted to life in this new and strange land. The Author of the Bible seems to have invested most of its narrative about this in the message that Israel became seduced by Canaanite religion and consequently fell prey to oppressors and needed to be rescued by Judges.

Summary: The Land that the Israelites entered at the beginning of the Times of the Judges was "off the screen" of the great empires of the day. There was official peace in the area and the city-states of Canaan were each on its own. The people who occupied the Land were of a radically different culture than the Israelites, though they were of similar genetic and linguistic stock. There was, for the Israelites, a great temptation to "respect the local gods" and to take part in that culture and religion, which no doubt looked to them to be more sophisticated and frankly more appealing than the austere Law that they were commanded to follow. Besides, it worked for the Canaanites, and they were now in Canaan.

It took a long time - - the Times of the Judges - - for Israel to restore themselves as a separated people devoted solely to the LORD, and even so they continually fell back into the Canaanite practices for another couple of centuries - - until the captivity in Babylon, hundreds of years later. After return from captivity, the Israelites or Jews learned, and they never again fell into idolatry. But that's a different story for a different book, the story of the Time Between the Testaments.

The Four Phases of
The Times of the Judges

For convenience, we will break the Times of the Judges into four parts: First, initial conquest; Second, a time of fighting off raiders; Third; the struggle with the Sea Peoples, including especially the Philistines; and Fourth; the establishment of the kingdom of David. These parts are not fully distinct and conditions overlapped among them.

We will cover these four phases in a chapter each in more detail than here. But as a preliminary orientation we need to relate those phases - - those periods of time - - to the persons and events in the Book of Judges.

It is well recognized that the sequence of stories in the Book of Judges is not exactly chronological. Some of the stories that come late in the book were in fact early in the period, and very likely some of the Judges were contemporary with each other because they judged only part of the total nation that was emerging. We can "correct" that sequence from related evidence in the stories, as will be mentioned in connection with each phase. The listing in Table 2 on the next page is a summary of the sequence that I propose.

Phase One, the initial occupation, began while Joshua was alive and leading the Israelites and is therefore not actually part of the Times of the Judges. However, we need to look at it closely because it is foundational to the actual times when Judges led. None of the Judges were active during the life of Joshua, although the first Judge, Othniel, was alive and was a leader before Joshua died. He did not become Judge until after Joshua's death.

Phase Two was one of fighting off raiders, encompassed the Judgeship of Othniel (Judges 3) as the first Judge. We know that he was first because he was the nephew and son-in-law of Caleb, Joshua's contemporary. And the

Table 2

JUDGES BY PHASE

PHASE	JUDGE or PERSON	ENEMY
PHASE ONE: INITIAL OCCUPATION	Othniel (pre-Judgeship)	Canaanite city of Debir 1250
PHASE TWO: INVASIONS	Othniel (as Judge)	Aramaeans
	Ehud	Moab
	Angry Levite	Tribe of Benjamin
	Gideon	Midian and Amelek
	Abimelek	Israselite city Shechim
	Tola	None
	Jair	None
PHASE THREE: SEA PEOPLES	Mikah / Young Levite	None
	Jephthah of Gilead	Philistines & Amon
	Deborah/Barak/Jael	Canaanite city Hazor
	Shamgar	Philistines
	Ibzan of Zebulon	None
	Elon of Zebulon	None
	Abdon of Zebulon	None
	Samson of Zorah/Mahaneh	Philistines
PHASE FOUR: ESTABLISHING THE KINGDOM	Samuel	Philistines

36

Times of the Judges come directly after the death of Joshua.

Table 2 lists the Judges and other characters who figure in the Book of Judges, with the enemies they opposed and arranged by their probable places in the four phases of this book.

At the beginning of Phase Two, Othniel was called to fight the Aramaeans of the northern Middle East. These particular Aramaeans were from Nahor in the area of northern Syria and northern Mesopotamia. As far as our records can tell us, this was the first outside attack on Israel, and it almost certainly came before the raid made by Pharaoh Merneptah about 1225 BC. (As is true of many events in Egyptian history, the surviving records allow for a lot of argument about dates. I've chosen this date as being most plausible to me. Others think otherwise.) Incidentally, there is no record in the Bible that a Judge was called to oppose the Pharaoh Merneptah..

Other Judges can be identified as belonging to the second phase because of the enemies they were called to oppose. Those enemies were the raiders who were active after Israel completed its first occupation and before the Sea Peoples (predominantly the Philistines) became the salient enemies of Israel. They define Phase Two and these enemies passed from prominence after 1185-1175 BC when the Sea Peoples invaded the Land.

Ehud (Judges 3) opposed Moab with its king Eglon. Moab was to the south of the Israelite territory that was east of the Jordan. Moab was assisted by Amon and Amelek. These assisting peoples lived east of the Jordan

River. Their presence gives testimony to the fact that Israel's occupation of the area east of the Jordan, territories that had were eventually assigned to the tribes of Ruben, Gad and half the tribe of Manasseh, were not yet fully consolidated into Israelite control.

[Shamgar (Judges 3) comes next in the text of the Book of Judges, but he does not belong in Phase Two, because his opponents were the Philistines. The Philistines were not in the Land until the beginning of Phase Three.]

The Angry Levite of Judges Chapters 19-21 is here listed as active in Phase Two because his actions resulted in the decimation of the tribe of Benjamin and the total destruction of the city of Gibeah. This set of events had to have taken place early in the Times in order for the tribe and city to recover as is related in Judges and in First Samuel. This Levite was not a Judge, of course, but he is a prominent character in the book. He and some other non-Judges are fictionalized in my companion book, *Judges, Rulers and One Angry Levite.* And he was indeed angry.

I list Gideon (Judges 6 – 8), Abimelek (Judges 9), Tola and Jair (Judges 10) as judging during Phase Two because the enemies they opposed were pre-Philistine. Recall that I have demarcated Phase Two from Phase Three by the advent of the Sea Peoples, who included the Philistines.

Phase Three, characterized by the depredations of the Philistines, begins with the invasion of the Sea Peoples. The Sea People who were most problematic to the Israelites were the Philistines. When their records refer to "the Philistines" the Israelites were no doubt blanketing in all of the Sea Peoples whom they encountered, as will be described in the chapter on Phase Three.

I place Micah (Judges 17 – 19) near the beginning of Phase Three. He was the young man who stole his mother's silver, repented, and made images that a young Levite in turn stole and took with the migrating tribe of Dan to the northern border of Canaan. The reason for placing him near the start of Phase Three is that the tribe of Dan seems to have been finally displaced when the Sea Peoples invaded into Dan's assigned territory.

Jephthah (Judges 10 – 12) is listed here because some of his opponents were Philistines.

Deborah, Barak and Jael (Judges 4 – 5) opposed the city-state of Hazor in northern Canaan. Since Hazor is usually counted as destroyed by Joshua within 20 years of Israel's entering Canaan, there had to take a considerable time for the city to again be a threat. Besides, the commanding general of Hazor, Sisera, had a name that indicates that he was probably one of the Sea Peoples.

Shamgar (Judges 3) "slew six hundred Philistines with an ox goad." This places him securely in Phase Three.

Ibzan, Elon and Abdon of Zebulon did not oppose any recorded enemies during their Judgeships. I place them in Phase Three mostly by default; the writer of the Book of Judges lists them in that part of the sequence. It is quite possible that they served during Phase Two. Interestingly, the allotment of the tribe of Zebulon was in an area that the Israelites did not fully conquer and where the Canaanites continued to dominate.

Samson (Judges 13 – 16) appears to be the last of the Judges except for Samuel. His struggles were with the Philistines at a time when the relationships between the Israelites and the Philistines had been stabilized.

Phase Four, the establishing of the Israelite kingdom under Saul and David, with the foundations laid by

Samuel, can be roughly dated from 1073 BC to 1000 BC. The only Judge during that period was Samuel, who was both the last Judge and the first Prophet. Not incidentally, he held other offices, including that of *de facto* High Priest. The Book of First Samuel, not the Book of Judges, records the Israelite events of Phase Four. My book, *Samuel, Seer*, gives a fictional autobiography of Samuel.

In summary, the phase divisions followed in this book are these.

> **Phase One**, from 1250 BC to about 1220 BC: the initial occupation. This is two to three decades.

> **Phase Two**, from about 1220 BC to about 1175 BC: a time of invasions by surrounding peoples. The two phases flow into each other. The conquest was still going on while the first Judges ruled. The entry of the Philistines and other Sea Peoples came in the middle of the Times of the Judges, and the Sea Peoples invaded about 1175 BC. So Phases One and Two took roughly 75 years, from about 1250 BC to 1175 BC.

> **Phase Three**, from about 1175 BC (when the Sea Peoples invaded) to about 1073 BC, when Samuel began to lay the foundations for a kingdom, a time of struggles against the Philistines. The entry of the Sea Peoples marks the division between Phases Two and Three; we'll get to those peoples later.

> **Phase Four**, from about 1073 BC to 1000 BC, the biarth of the kingdom with Samuel acting as midwife.

These, then, are the convenient four phases into which we can divide the Times of the Judges. Let us consider each of them in a separate chapter and in more detail.

First Phase: Initial Occupation

You will recall that the great empires did not oppose Israel when it entered Canaan. The international situation was quiet.

The conquest of Canaan by Israel was an extended process. The initial part evidently took decades and was not fully completed until King David finally subdued the Philistines. Thus, the Times of the Judges were times of increasing occupation of the Land. The occupation was gradual and by no means a lightning war.

The date for entry of Israel into Canaan I've chosen is 1250 BC. Recall that there is argument about the date, but my best belief is 1250 BC or very close to it. The Israelites are said by many historians to have burned Hazor about 1230 BC. That would give two decades for the earliest conquest.

The first phase, that of initial conquest, lasted many years. In a real sense, the conquest was not completed until the end of Phase Four, the time of King David. Even then the occupation was composed both of literal occupation and of domination of subject peoples by Israel rather than by complete displacement of the Canaanites.

Figure 4 shows the main paths of the Israelite invasion of Canaan. Along the way they encountered various peoples who are shown along the right side of the map. Arrows point to their general locations. The path of Israel is shown by a branching arrow.

Note that the initial conquest of Greater Canaan began before the entry into Canaan west of the Jordan, and it is described in the Book of Joshua. We are used to thinking that the conquest began with the fall of the walls of Jericho. But if we go back a bit, we find that Israel had already conquered and occupied Trans-Jordan, the land we now call the western part of the nation of Jordan and

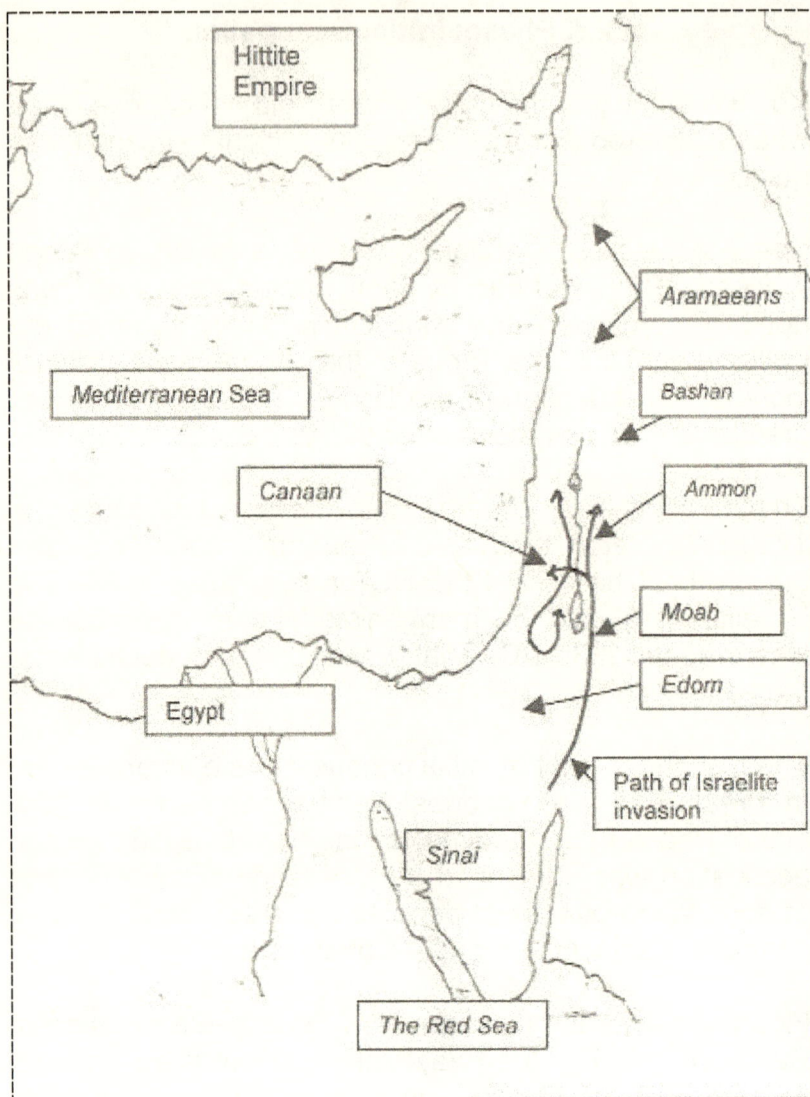

Hittite
Empire

Aramaeans

Mediterranean Sea

Bashan

Canaan

Ammon

Moab

Edom

Egypt

Path of Israelite
invasion

Sinai

The Red Sea

Fig. 4
The Israelite invasion of Canaan
about 1250 BC

the Golan Heights claimed by Syria. This is the territory east of the Jordan River, and its inclusion makes for Greater Canaan. It was occupied at the time of the Exodus by peoples or territories named Moabites, Bashan, Gilead, Jezer, Heshbon, and the like. These territories had been taken by Israel on its way to Canaan proper. When preparations were made for the assault on Jericho, Israel left that eastern part of their Land to the women and children of the tribes of Reuben, Gad, and half the tribe of Menasseh. After the conquest of Canaan west of the Jordan the men of those tribes returned and settled in this hospitable area. At least it looked hospitable to them at that time. In modern times much of it is deforested and eroded and barren, but then it was attractive to the Israelites.

The initial conquest did not all go smoothly. There were defeats as well as victories, and one city-state (Gibeah) tricked Israel into enslaving it rather than destroying it. By and large, though, Israel's spread throughout Canaan was irresistible. It just was not complete. Some city-states, notably Jebus (later known as Jerusalem) were defeated in the field of battle but the city itself was not actually taken; the Jebusites continued to hold Jebus until the time of David.

The entry into Canaan east of the Jordan through Jericho, into Canaan as we usually think of it, is well known. The Israelite encampment during the "fall of the walls of Jericho" was then just north of the city, at Gilgal in the Jordan Valley. Gilgal was the base of operations for a time, and perhaps the Israelite noncombatants stayed there while the army went on campaign.

The charge to Israel in Canaan west of the Jordan was quite straightforward. Israel had instructions to occupy the land and exterminate the occupants, the Canaanites. This they set out to do.

Jericho fell, and its inhabitants, except for the family of Rahab, were killed. Then Ai was attacked, a defeat for Israel because of disobedience by one of its families. This was dealt with, and Ai fell.

In the next sentence, the Book of Joshua has Israel at Mount Ebal, far up the country half the way from the Dead Sea to the Sea of Galilee. They could not have gotten there unless they had quieted the small cities between Ai and Ebal. The route was a long-established trade road and this may have facilitated the movement. It may have been an expedition to the place that Moses had commanded them to visit, rather than a true part of the conquest of Canaan. Joshua may or may not have left a part of the army in that area, but we next read that Joshua was back at Gilgal.

The Canaanites had seen what Israel was setting about to do. Not only was Israel openly intending to exterminate or exile them, but it was clear that Israel's LORD was powerful enough to give them fairly consistent victory. As was true of all the peoples of that day, there was no doubt as to where power came from; it came from the god of a people, and Israel was a people whose god was not bound to the land like the gods of the other nations. Until now, it was understood that a god had power in his own territory, so there was a Baal of Peor, a Baal of Tyre, and Baals of other places. There were national gods, such as Chemosh of the Moabites and Marduk of the Assyrians. All those gods stayed in one place and was thought of as having concern only for their particular peoples. Now here was a "portable god," the LORD of the Israelites, who traveled with them and exerted His power wherever they went. And evidently He was more powerful than the local gods of the people whom He overwhelmed.

To the Canaanites, the choice was stark: find a way not to be defeated, or be exterminated. Some individuals may have migrated northwest into the area north of Tyre that we call Phoenicia but that then was indistinguishable culturally from Canaan.

Slavish submission was preferable to death, and the Hivites of Gibeah tricked Israel into letting them live in exchange for becoming servants. (I think that this Gibeah or Gibeon was the same as the Gibeah of Saul, though there is some debate over this.)

Other Canaanites rightly viewed this "surrender" of the Gibeonites as a defection of an important component of any resistance that had to be mounted against Israel. They had to rouse themselves to defend their land.

The Lord of Jebus, the City of Peace (the word for peace is Salem), Adoni or Lord Salem, gathered around him the armed forces of four other city-states to punish Gibeah. Here we have the first organized resistance to Israel, though Adoni Salem was careful to attack only Gibeah and probably thought he might avoid confronting Israel directly. The now-subjected Gibeonites appealed to Joshua back at Gilgal for help, and the decisive fight for southern Canaan was on. Israel marched all night up to Gibeah in the hill country and surprised the armies of the five city-states while they were still outside the fortress of Gibeah.

The outcome was that the five kings were defeated and executed and their armies were killed almost to the man, the LORD hurling large hailstones on them as they fled.

For good measure, Israel went on to destroy the cities of the four kings who had joined Adoni Salem: Hebron, Debir, Eglon and Lachish. But the fortifications of Jebus or Jerusalem were too tough to crack, and it was left on its ridge above the Kidron Valley. Its king and its army had been destroyed.

Israel made a loop south of Jebus and back to Gilgal. So the southern part of Canaan was reduced to submission, though we don't have a record that this submission extended to the seacoast. From subsequent events we infer that most of the natives were not exterminated by Israel. They remained as peoples among whom the Israelites would settle. Israel was established in the southern hill country, in the southern Jordan Valley, probably in the desert south of Jebus, and in the territory east of the Jordan.

Northern Canaan reacted much as had the south. The city-states united under the leadership of one of its greatest cities, Hazor. At that time Hazor was a very considerable city and had dominated the area for centuries. Its situation was not as commercially favorable as was that of Megiddo, which controlled the intersection of two large trade routes. However, Hazor did control the trade route that led from Egypt to Damascus, and it had the advantage of a large and well-fortified hill.

The king of Hazor, Jabin, bore a name that will turn up maybe a hundred years later in the Book of Judges. It must have been a dynastic title for the king of Hazor rather than a personal name. He gathered a very large army, greater than that of Adoni Salem of Jerusalem, with both foot troops and chariots. As far as we know this would be Israel's first encounter with chariots since those of Pharaoh were drowned in the Reed Sea.

The war chariot was the tank of ancient warfare. When it had been introduced to the Middle East some 500 years earlier it had revolutionized warfare. Different armies used the chariot differently. The Mycenaean Greeks of that time seem to have used the chariot to drive to the battle, then to dismount and fight on foot. The Egyptians had light chariots with a driver and a fighter who was equipped with sword and spear but whose primary weapon was the bow. The heavier Hittite chariot had a driver and two fighters, and the Egyptians wrote that this was unfair. In all cases the chariot was drawn by two horses, and the horses had no collars (a device that in its

46

turn would much later revolutionize agriculture because it enables a horse to use its full strength). Instead, the horses wore yokes over their necks and pulled against breastbands that restricted their breathing, so the chariot had to be light.

It was demoralizing for foot troops to be charged by those large, snorting and whinnying animals with their flashing hoofs, amid the screaming and dust clouds of battle. A chariot charge could break most lines of foot soldiers.

(In my fictional book *Judges, Rulers and One Angry Levite*, I have Barak destroy a chariot charge by using an elementary and obvious tactic, aided by the boggy ground onto which he enticed them.)

Israel again took the initiative and fell upon the Canaanites with the assurance from the LORD that they would win. The Canaanites were again defeated and were given no quarter. The instructions to the Israelites were to kill all the men, women and children. Hazor was burned, but subsequent events in the time of the Judge Deborah show that it was resettled by Canaanites. The archaeological traces of that resettlement are not substantial, however.

After the defeat of the Hazor confederacy the Israelites burned the chariots. Such things were of no use to them. They also hamstrung the horses. In those days, a horse was almost exclusively a military machine. A horse was no good to a civilian because a farmer plowed with oxen or by hand-powered mattock. If the horses were hamstrung in the heat of battle, that would be only good tactics because one hamstrung horse would disable the chariot and would turn it into an entangling obstacle to the other chariots. But if the horses were hamstrung after the battle, as the Bible seems to say, one hopes that the horses were then humanely killed. A hamstrung horse would die of thirst if infection or the inevitable post-battle scavenging animals didn't get it first. Unlike most

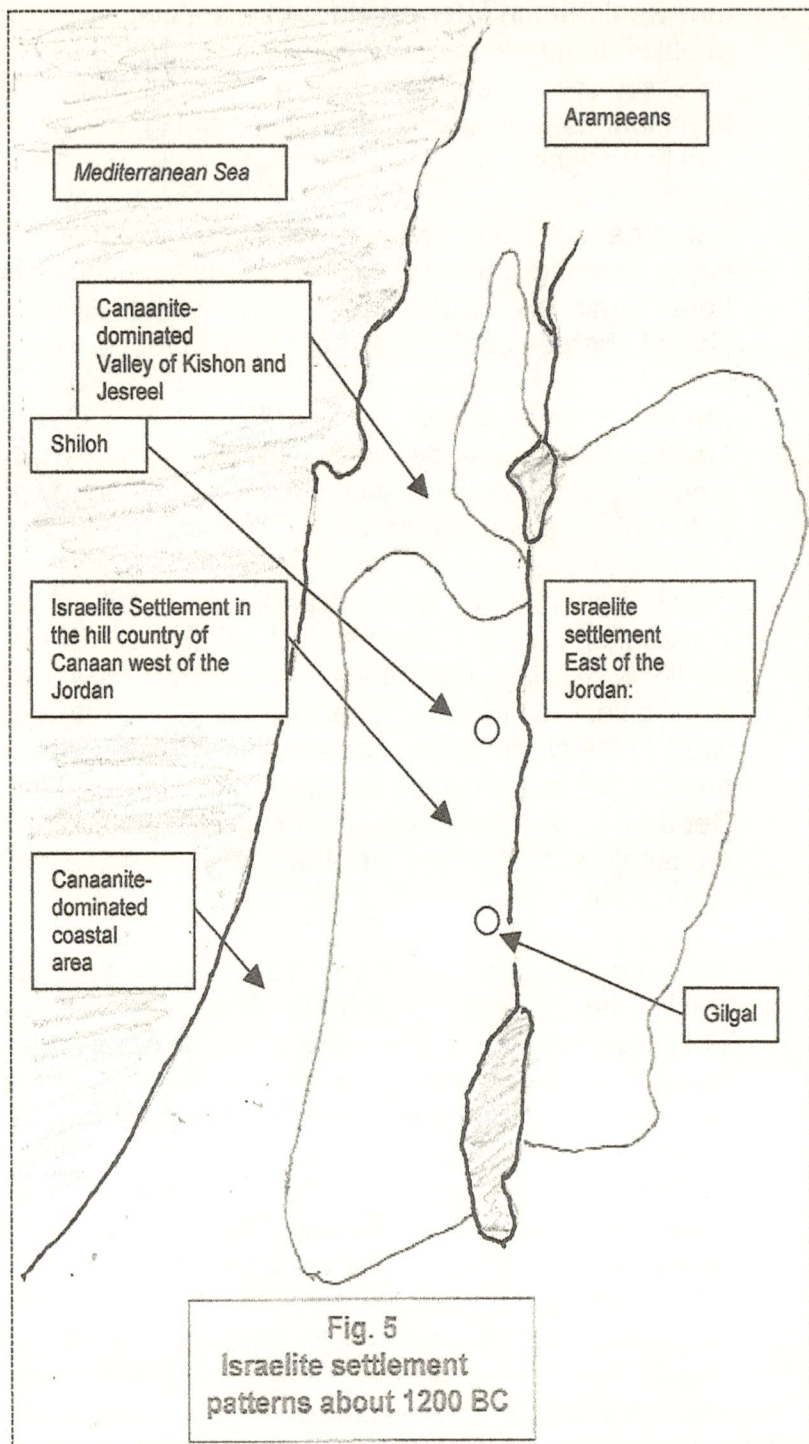

Aramaeans

Mediterranean Sea

Canaanite-
dominated
Valley of Kishon and
Jesreel

Shiloh

Israelite Settlement in
the hill country of
Canaan west of the
Jordan

Israelite
settlement
East of the
Jordan:

Canaanite-
dominated
coastal
area

Gilgal

Fig. 5
Israelite settlement
patterns about 1200 BC

animals, a horse cannot run or even stand for any period on three legs. It is strictly an open-land animal, built to run, and to run on all four legs.

All the towns of Canaan were destroyed by Israel – except that the cities on mounds, the cities that were fortified, were not destroyed and their people survived. When the killing was over these Canaanites emerged and became the neighbors of the Israelites. The settlements that were too small to be fortified but were smart enough and obscure enough to be overlooked may have had survivors also. In any case, the first phase of occupation, up to the death of Joshua, ended with many Canaanites still in possession of the Land.

The Book of Joshua ends with chapters that point out the failure of Israel to exterminate the Canaanites. Some of the remaining areas would not be conquered until the time of David, two hundred or more years later. One large swath of Canaanite remnant was from the Jordan Valley east of Beth Shean, along the fertile Kishon and Jezreel Valleys north of Mount Carmel on the trade route to the Mediterranean, and to the coast at the modern cities of Acco and Haifa. For that matter, Israel's occupation of the southeast Mediterranean coastal plain was not completed or secure until the time of David.

Figure 5 shows the pattern of Israelite settlement after the conquest. You will note that the valley of the Kishon and Jesreel as well as the coastal plain were not really occupied by Israel, nor would they be until the time of David.

The recorded speeches of Joshua as he declared the tribal allotments sound rather petulant. The tribes complain that they don't have enough territory. Joshua says, in effect, "Look, all this land is yours. Go up and drive out the Canaanites, clear the forests, and settle the land that is given to you. How long will you wait? Quit complaining and get to work."

49

But "the Canaanites were determined to live in their land," as the Book of Joshua records. The result was that the Land was mixed Israelite and Canaanite, with all the consequent temptations of Israel to become one with the Canaanites.

The Israelites remained faithful to the LORD while Joshua and his companions lived. Then began Phase Two, and Israel was attacked by outsiders as well as being infiltrated by Canaanite culture.

Second Phase: Oppressions

The empires of Egypt and the Hittites ignored the Israelite conquest of Canaan. At any rate, they did not intervene, though Egypt was still nominally responsible for the Land.

Phase Two opened with a mixed settlement. The Israelites had conquered the Land but had not occupied all of it. There were remaining pockets of resistant Canaanites. Those Canaanites who had been conquered but who still lived in the Land were supposed to have been reduced to servants of Israel – in those days, equivalent to slavery. It is not at all certain from the record that they and the Israelites knew that the Canaanites were slaves, but that was the assumption written into the Book. They may not all have been actually subjected.

It is also possible that, as time went on, the conqueror-subject contract was less and less enforced. The Canaanites probably were subject to levies of forced labor at the will of the Israelite tribe to whom they were in service. But they lived.

The Law did not require non-Israelites to follow the commands given to Moses, so the Canaanites continued to practice their religion. Perhaps the Israelites interpreted the command to consider themselves a special people to mean that a non-Israelite was positively forbidden to follow the Law. We don't know. The Law put serious barriers in the way of any Canaanite being accepted into the Israelite religion and culture.

There was certainly some cultural mixing. As best we can tell in the absence of statements to the contrary, after the killing ended the Canaanites continued as they were except for the forced labor. The Israelites were newcomers to the Land, undertaking a way of life that they had not known before. They had had four hundred years of dependence in Egypt and forty years of desert wandering with food (manna) supplied. Then they had had a couple of decades of living off the land, appropriating the grain, flocks, clothing, houses and wine of the natives they were fighting. Now the fighting was over and there was no longer a dependable outside source of food, shelter and clothing. They had to go to work and make a living in the new Land. Their only examples of how to do that were the Canaanites.

The interaction between Israel and the religion(s) of the Canaanites fits the pattern that prevails whenever a desert people encounter a farming people. Religious seduction continued throughout the four phases of the Times of the Judges, and it continued also after the establishment of the Kingdom of David and up to the time of the scattering of the Northern Kingdom by Assyria and the captivity of Judah by Babylon. The seduction began as soon as Israel entered Canaan.

Though the Canaanites basically were a settled agricultural people, they also kept flocks. The Israelites were, at the time they entered Canaan, a desert people dependent mostly on shepherding with the complicating factor that they had been dependent upon manna instead of upon grain. They were familiar with grain at least to the extent of using it in religious ceremonies, but they could not raise it while they wandered in the desert.

So here we have the entry into a farming country by a people who were unfamiliar with farming. Recall that of the thousands of men who left Egypt only two, Joshua and Caleb, were still alive when Israel entered Canaan. They, and only they, had seen farms before the glancing encounter of migrating Israel with the sown lands east of Jordan. Israel would continue to keep flocks of sheep and goats but it also had to become dependent on raising grains, olives for oil, and grapes. The Israelites would have had no idea of how to become farmers.

Canaanite religion was inextricably bound into farming. The god invoked most often was Baal or the Baals ("Ba'alim" is the plural in Canaanite and Hebrew). The sexual temple rites, done openly and with participation by the farmers, were what we call "sympathetic magic." The rites were not like our Christmas pageants. They were not just "plays" to remind and instruct people. They were actions that were believed to actually cause the farm cycle to take place. If the people enacted fertility, then the gods would be fertile. If the gods were fertile, then the fields would be fertile. Canaanites believed that if they did not act out the sacred ritual of fertility, fertility of the fields would not result.

If an Israelite were to ask a Canaanite farmer, "How do you do this farming thing?" the Canaanite would probably reply, "Well, you're dependent upon Baal for the germination of the seed and especially for the rain you'll need. So you have to give offerings to Baal and worship him properly. And the essential thing you have to do in order for the crop cycle to run is that you have to hold this fertility ceremony at the temple. Then you have to support the temple priestesses and patronize them sexually as often as you can. Oh yes, and you have to sow seed in this way, and take out these plants we call weeds, and keep the birds and animals out of the grain, and of course harvest and thresh and store it this way, and save your seeds for next year. We recognize other gods, too, but Baal is the one who gives us our crops. You can't farm without him."

Were it not for the commands in the Law, the Israelite would have no way to see any other means of successful farming. There was powerful temptation to copy the successful farming practices of the Canaanites, Baal and all. If you don't know how to farm and if you need to farm, you ask a successful farmer, and the Canaanites were successful enough to be pretty impressive and influential teachers. When the Philistines came later, they had no Law and they adopted the Canaanite gods.

The warnings of Moses and Joshua had been clear. If the Israelites fell into the religious practices of the heathen, then they would be prey to enemies.

Shortly after the conquest, and actually overlapping it in time, came the events that called into being the Judges in response to attacks by indigenous people and by neighboring peoples. In this second phase that we are discussing, the enemies of Israel were peoples native to the Levant who either invaded from a nearby location or who infiltrated the Land as nomads. Only later in Phase Three would a new people, the Sea Peoples personified by the Philistines, be the enemy.

Because of their stubbornness the Israelites had been warned at the beginning of the 40-year wandering of the Exodus that no one over age 20 then alive would enter Canaan. Two men did: Joshua and Caleb. Joshua would take over the leadership from Moses. Caleb had his own inheritance in Canaan, but he had to go in and claim it by force. And he had a nephew who we can confidently claim to be the first of the Judges.

This first Judge, Othniel (Judges 3), was a hero of one of the city conflicts. His uncle Caleb ceded to him the Canaanite city of Debir by virtue of Othniel's conquest of that city. Othniel in later years became a Judge. Hence we know that this second phase of the Times of the Judges began maybe 30 years after the entry into the Land and the fall of Jericho.

At the time of Othniel, the Israelites were not the only peoples who were on the move. A long period of restlessness had begun, to be culminated in the invasion of the Sea Peoples. We don't know what it was that impelled this surging of peoples around the eastern Mediterranean. Perhaps it was a time of drought or other climatic stress. At any rate, at about this time the usual testing of borders became more pronounced. Far to the north, the Assyrians, who had been relegated to the role of buffer between the Hittites and the Babylonians, began to stir. The Hittite Empire had begun to falter and to look inward, and the Babylonians were similarly weak. The Assyrian king, Tiglath-Pileser I, pushed south against the Aramaeans. In turn, the Aramaeans of Syria and upper Mesopotamia pushed south. There they encountered the Canaanites and the Israelites. The Book of Judges records that the Aramaean king Cushan-Rishathaim established military and economic control over Israel. This Aramaean king oppressed Israel for eight years.

He or other Arameans also pushed back against the Assyrians, and with such success that Assyria entered into another century of decline.

In Israel, Othniel became Judge and he led a successful war against the Aramaeans. We are not told how he accomplished this, though in my fictional book, *Judges, Rulers, and One Angry Levite,* I hypothesize that he organized a rolling, secret massing of Israel to meet Cushan-Rishathaim and forced him to relinquish his hold on Israel-Canaan. This was the first of the recorded conflicts that arose after Israel was settled in the Land.

The major conflicts are shown in Figure 6. The probable invasion paths of Israel's enemies are shown. In addition, the map shows two conflicts that took place within Israel itself, at Shechem (the protagonist was Abimelech in Judges Chapter 9) and at Gibeah (the initiating character was the Angry Levite of Judges 19-21).

The contest between the Aramaean Cushan and the Assyrians would occupy Cushan enough so that he would not return to press Israel. The Aramaeans seem to have henceforth abandoned their push to the south, but to have instead settled into stable kingdoms in northern Mesopotamia that lasted hundreds of years.

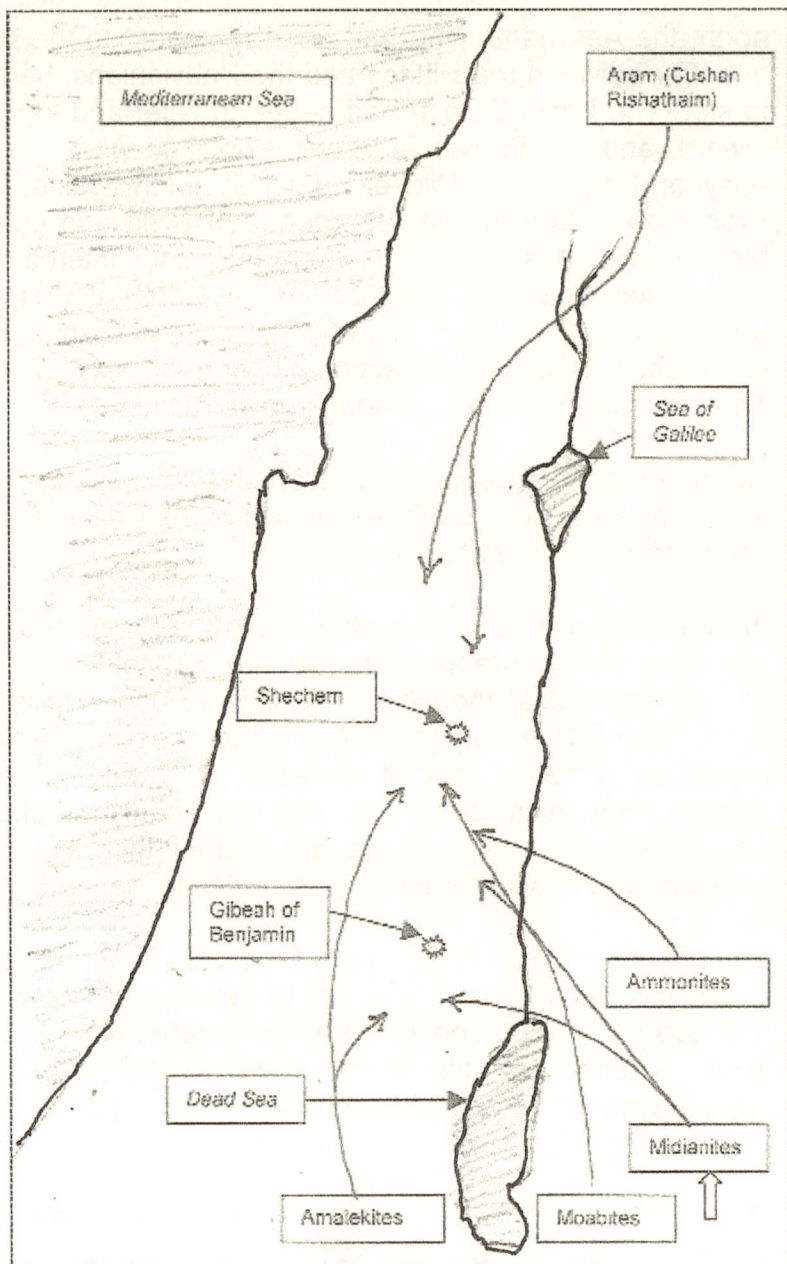

Mediterranean Sea

Aram (Cushan Rishathaim)

Sea of Galilee

Shechem

Gibeah of Benjamin

Ammonites

Dead Sea

Midianites

Amalekites

Moabites

Fig. 6
Enemies, invasions and internal conflicts
Prior to Sea Peoples' Invasions, 1230 to
1175 BC

Israel next was assailed by Moab, the country east and south of the Dead Sea. How the Moabites invaded and how much territory they conquered in Canaan is not told. However, the Moabites, led by their king Eglon, conquered Jericho and its valuable spring of fresh water, and he enlisted the Ammonites and Amalekites to join with him in dominating the Land.

Because there were few fixed borders, and because of the common tendency to name a diverse people (especially enemies) after the most prominent component of them, our records of what peoples lived where are a bit uncertain. Even now there is not complete agreement among scholars as to exactly where some of the peoples lived. It appears that the Ammonites lived just east of the territory assigned to the Israelite tribe of Gad, east of the Jordan, and that their headquarters were what is now the Jordanian capitol of Amman. They may also have co-occupied part of the Gad territory, since at that time Israel had not fully consolidated its control over Canaan.

The Amalekites were more nomadic residents of the desert southwest of the Dead Sea, and their economy was camel-based. These two "nations" were not really under the control of Moab, but rather seem to have been allowed by him to be opportunistic raiders of a country (Israel) that had no central control of its own. This sort of raiding was common in the Middle East until modern times.

The Judge who was raised to oppose Moab was Ehud (Judges 3). He was a Benjamite, from the tribe whose territory was just north of Jerusalem. Because of his prominence in the story we can infer that this took place before the tribe of Benjamin was decimated in the internal Israelite warfare touched off by the Angry Levite of Judges 19 - 21. Ehud was strategically correct in attacking Eglon, king of Moab, because this cut the invasion off at its head, leaving the Ammonites and Amalekites without Moab's protection and allowing Israel to expel them.

Suddenly without a king and with no plan in place for succession to the throne, Moab temporarily dissolved in internal struggles. Ehud led a punitive expedition into Moab to terminate Moab's oppression.

So, as we have seen, Israel was invaded early in its occupation of the Land by invaders first from the north and then from the east and south.

Invaders were not the only problem. We have seen that the Israelites were enticed into apostasy by living among the Canaanites and their religion. The Book of Judges keeps repeating that apostasy was followed by oppression. It was also accompanied by intertribal conflict. The Angry Levite (Judges 19 – 21) epitomizes this ongoing danger of internal strife over a moral issue. It was one of the most damaging episodes, one that nearly wiped out one of the twelve tribes, and it was precipitated without outside oppression.

In this episode, the rape of a Levite's concubine in the city of Gibeah caused the Levite to incite all of Israel to assemble to take vengeance. When the city refused to yield up the rapists and the city's tribe (Benjamin) supported it, the other Israelites killed out all of the tribe except 600 men. This episode had to have been early in the Times of the Judges in order for Benjamin and Gibeah to recover enough to produce Israel's first king, Saul of Gibeah.

One famous Judge was, however, the leader in the struggle against an external oppressor. That man was Gideon (Judges 6 – 8).

The oppressors were again the camel-based nomads who originated in the southern deserts of Sinai and Arabia, the Midianites and again the Amalekites. The nature of this kind of oppression is seldom that of the imposition of a foreign government. Nomads are generally not interested in establishing institutions. They simply descend like locusts and raid for loot.   That they were able to thus dominate Israel is explained by the fact that Israel had no civil government and consisted of non-united tribes.   No effective defense could be mounted until a Judge (Gideon) was raised who could rally a multi-tribal force sufficient to cause the raiders to come together to fight him.   The resulting Battle of the Lamp Jars needs no repetition here. See Judges Chapters 6 to 8. The raiders were repelled with sufficient losses, and with pursuit out of the Land, to deter them from returning.

Not all the leaders cited in the Book of Judges are recorded as struggling against external or internal enemies. Gideon's son Abimelek of the city of Shechem (Judges 9), while not a Judge in any usual sense, is a prominent figure in the Book of Judges. His struggle was internal and it would be hard to find the value of that struggle to the establishment of Israel.   Two actual Judges, Tola and Jair (Judges 10), seem to have fulfilled their Judgeships in Phase Two; they are not said to have any enemies.   Perhaps that lack of deliverance from enemies was the reason that we were not given much information about Tola and Jair.

It is probable that, by the end of Phase Two (about 1130 BC), Israel had consolidated its control of the Land enough to discourage easy raiding by neighboring peoples.   The remaining Canaanites were subdued although still influential. It must have seemed to Israel that it had successfully inherited Canaan and that now everything would be stable.

It was not to be.

Third Phase: Contesting with the Philistines

About 1185 to 1175 BC an event occurred which radically changed the Eastern Mediterranean. A mixed host, the Sea Peoples, invaded through what is now Turkey and along the adjacent sea-lanes. They came with their families and carts and cattle, rolling like a wave through land and harbor. It was a mass migration, accompanied by the ruin of whole civilizations, including the extinction of writing systems such as those of the Hittites and the Cypro-Minoans.

The foreshadow of the invasion had taken place in the previous century, when Pharaoh Rameses II defeated a first wave of Sherden. The first Trojan War (there were two, and this first one is said to have taken place about 1250 BC, while Israel was entering Canaan) seems also to have been part of the beginning, though full development of the invasion took over 75 years. In about 1175 BC the main thrust of the Sea Peoples hit the Levant.

Two events – the death of the powerful Pharaoh Rameses II and later the fall of the Hittite empire – seem to have eventually unplugged the building tide of what we know as the Sea Peoples, and an unrest that had been rising for some time became a migration.

The term, "Sea Peoples," is an unavoidable problem. This is the title that is almost universally applied to them. But they were not a single people, and they were by no means all from the sea. We will have to live with the term anyway.

The region of the eastern and northern Mediterranean had always had conflict except for the 70 years of the Hittite–Egyptian treaty. For the previous few hundred years of which we have any evidence, peoples were pushing their neighbors. Much of this may have been peaceful as

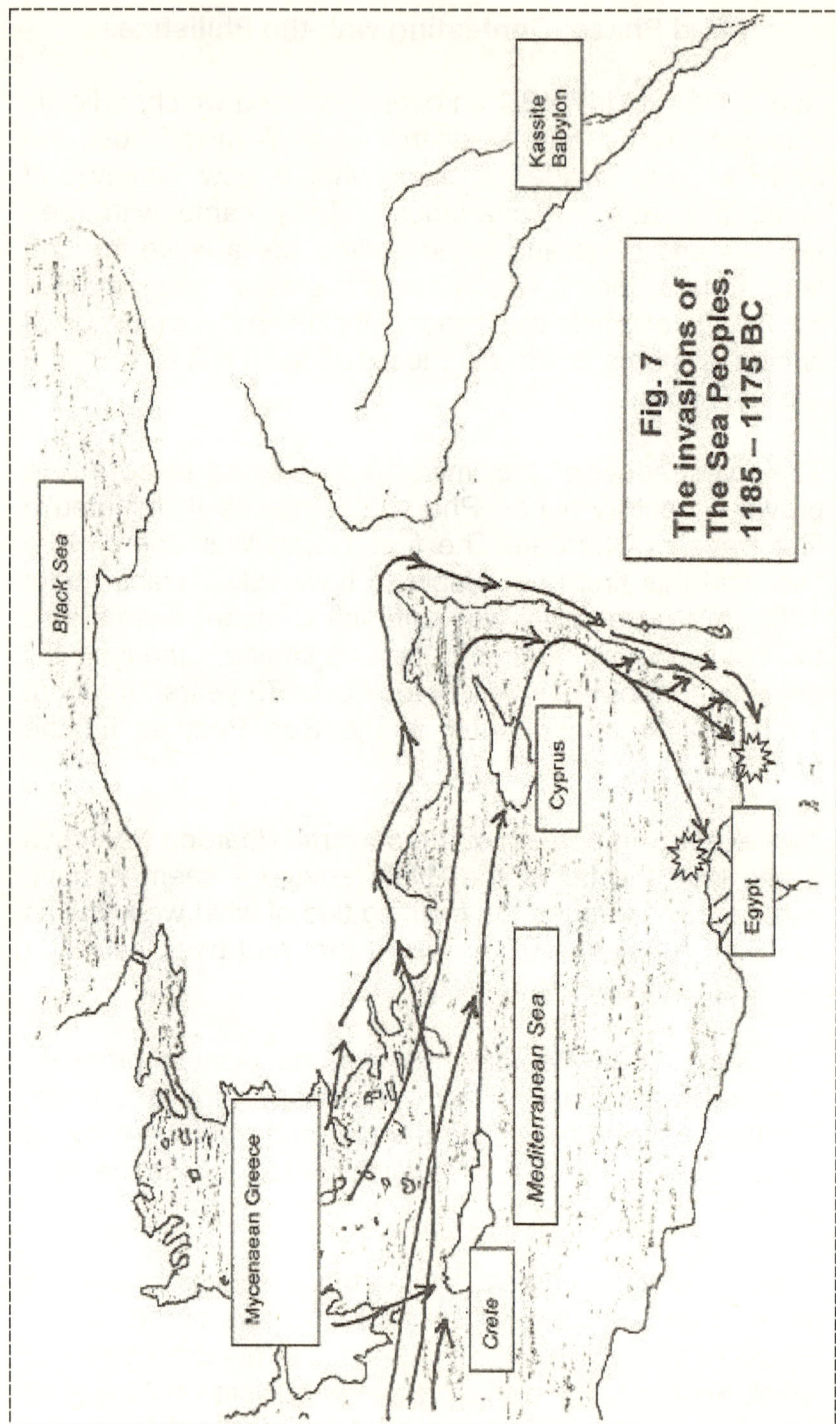

Fig. 7
The invasions of
The Sea Peoples,
1185 – 1175 BC

Kassite Babylon

Black Sea

Cyprus

Egypt

Mediterranean Sea

Mycenaean Greece

Crete

groups moved into sparsely populated areas, but more seems to have consisted of aggressive raids and displacement and conquest of less aggressive populations. The Greeks appear to have moved into their peninsula and islands some centuries earlier, transforming Greece into the Mycenaean coalition of city-states. And these Mycenaeans, whom we know as Homer's Greeks, then took over a highly cultured civilization in Crete and adopted a veneer of Cretan culture. They even invented ways to write words in early Greek, but never went beyond lists to write true literature – their poetry was chanted orally and was only written down three centuries later. By 1300 BC the Greeks had extended their dominance to Crete and even Cyprus, the big island in the northeast corner of the Mediterranean Sea with its treasure trove of copper ore that supported the late Bronze Age.

On the mainland, the Aramaeans had pushed the Ammonites southward to Syria and the Golan where Joshua met them. Far to the east, beyond the area of Babylon and therefore not noticeable to the Israelites, the Elamites were invading the Kassite-ruled Babylonian kingdom.

All these skirmishes prior to the 12th Century BC were rendered trivial by what happened next.

The starting place and the cause of the movement are not known, nor do we know with certainty all the participants. What we know is that in the 12th Century BC the whole of the eastern half of the north coast of the Mediterranean Sea began to move. The movement was so large that it took decades to drift to a halt. A wave of peoples began to move eastward, then south along the east coast of the Mediterranean Sea.

Figure 7 shows the main thrusts of the invasion. Not all of the known routes can be shown, because so much of the population was on the move. Some of the peoples came from west of the limits of the map in Figure 7, from the west coast of what is now Italy and from what are now Sicily and Sardinia.

The second Trojan War, the one that Homer sang about, was probably a part of the movement. Such a war actually took place, though perhaps the details we have are fictional. As best we can tell, the second and final Trojan War took place near 1100 BC. Also near that time, the Hittite empire was destroyed, as were the Mycenaean Greek city-states. One version of the Greek history is that a new Greek people, the Dorians, swept over the Mycenaeans and destroyed their fortified cities. Or it may have been a revolt of the peasants after the more vigorous Mycenaeans left on migration with the Sea Peoples. Or both. At any rate, Greece entered into its dark age and social chaos engulfed the whole area.

The non-Hittite people who lived west of the Hittites in Anatolia (modern Turkey), the Phrygians and Luvians, moved eastward and invaded clear over into upper Mesopotamia and into Syria. They were probably responsible for the final destruction of the Hittite Empire. For the sake of simplicity they are not shown on the map of Figure 7. Behind them or with them came a host of other peoples with names that do not always betray where they came from: Sherdan, Weshesh, Sicals or Shekelesh, the Teresh or Tyrshenoi, the Ekwesh, the Lukka, the Denen, and of course the "plst" or Peleset or Peleshti or Philistines. (See Appendix B for help in sorting out these obscure peoples.)

There is a great deal of argument as to where the whole bunch did come from. Here, I will hew pretty closely to the theory that they came from many places along, as well as inland from, the east half of the north coast of the Mediterranean.

As to their individual identity during the migration, we are secure in the identification of the "plst" (Egyptians had no written vowels) or Peleset or Peleshti as the Philistines. The best guess as to their origin is that they were related to the Mycenaean Greeks or contained elements of them, and that they came through Cyprus. The Philistines were the most prominent of the Sea Peoples who settled on the coast of Canaan and who plagued the Israelites. And, apart from the inscriptions of the Egyptians, it was the Israelites who wrote down the account of the Sea Peoples that we are most familiar with. They seem to have called all of the Sea Peoples Philistines.

The Lukka seem to have been the Lycians of western Anatolia. The Ekwesh (Ahiyawasha in the Hittite language) probably were the Achaeans of Homer's Greece. They may have joined into or even transformed into the Philistines; at least they shared cultural elements. The Denen similarly were probably Homer's Danoi Greeks. The Sherdan are thought by many to be from Sardinia and the Sheklesh from Sicily. The Teresh or Tursha or Tyrshenoi are thought to be the Eturuscans of northwest Italy. All these names may be misleading us, of course, because the chroniclers of that time tended to report events with the supposition that their readers would know the background. The things that "everyone knows," such as just who those peoples were, were left unrecorded. Further you will recall that neither the Egyptians nor the Israelites wrote with vowels, so we have only the consonants to go on. ("plst" for "Philistine" is a good example.) But the foregoing is the best we can reconstruct. In addition there were no doubt smaller unnamed groups who were swept up in the great folk movement.

This was not like the invasion of an army which had a home base and which was going to raid, loot and subjugate a new land and keep the home base. This was, like the invasion of the Israelites themselves, the migration of whole populations that were spearheaded by

65

warriors.   The best conclusion is that there were huge movements of whole peoples under way.

As is usual in history the more conservative or timid members of a nation would stay home and the more aggressive and hardy and perhaps reckless members would take to the road.   The fate of those who stayed home would range from impoverishment to eventual rise to a new national identity.   Thus the Greeks who stayed home took centuries to recover from their dark age, while the stay-at-home Etruscans (assuming that the Teresh were Etruscans) continued to dominate northwest Italy until Rome rose to power.

It must have seemed to the Egyptians and the nations along the eastern coast of the Mediterranean -- and to the Israelites -- that the whole world was falling upon them in a devouring flood.   The saving grace for the Israelites was that they were mostly in the highlands, away from the coastal plain where the invasion primarily played out.

Not all Israelites were safe in the mountains and the Jordan Valley and beyond.   The tribe of Dan had been allotted the part of the coastal plain where the Philistines and other Sea Peoples settled.   Dan had trouble settling there from the first because of the well-fortified cities and the prosperity of the coastal Canaanites.   The tribe of Manasseh north of them and the tribe of Judah south of them could pull back into the uplands, but Dan could not. From subsequent events we can infer that some Danites moved south into the Judah territory (the Danite Samson lived in a town that had been assigned to Judah) and some moved north and conquered a city that had not been allotted to Israel at all, the city then called Laish and which they renamed Dan.

This sideshow of Dan is reflected not only in Samson (Judges 13 – 16) but also in the story of Micah, his mother and his Levite, and the migration led by Dan's army (Judges 17 – 18).   It may also be behind the obscure reference to Dan abiding by its ships (Judges 5:17). If Dan had previously established itself at all on the seacoast, it would naturally have depended partly upon shipping. But the inferred story of Dan is not central to the interaction of Israel with the Sea Peoples as represented by the Philistines. The remainder of the Book of Judges and First Samuel is pretty well focused upon all Israel's struggles with the Philistines.

What kind of people were the Philistines? We have many indications in the Bible and elsewhere, even though we have a great many unanswered questions about them.

The Egyptians pictured them as warriors with round shields, long straight swords, and helmets distinguished by a crown of upright red feathers or fiber. They fought in much the same way as did the Greeks of Homer. A champion would first challenge someone to come out and fight him alone (think Achilles and Goliath), insulting the opposition and boasting of what he would do. The Philistine would fit himself with particular armor (compare Goliath's outfit with Achilles arming himself in the Iliad) and begin the fight with a spear.

The Israelites appear to have referred to all Sea Peoples as Philistines. This is similar to what the English of 1100 years ago did with the Viking invaders, whom they called Danes. It was immaterial to the English that most of the Vikings came from Norway and others came from Sweden and Denmark. The king of the ones they saw in southern England was a Dane, so all Vikings were Danes to them. Who cared to be exact about names when the sword was upon them? To the Israelites, all Sea Peoples were Philistines. And true it is that most of the Sea Peoples on the coast of Israel were Philistines.

Like the Greeks and indeed like many peoples of the day, the Philistines respected and adopted the gods of the area they settled in. They may have picked up Dagon as they came down from the north, though Dagon worship was already somewhat established in the coastal plain of Palestine (It is called Palestine because the Romans gave the Philistine's name to the country some centuries later). They honored the local Baals as well.

The Philistines did not write, as far as we know. By the time of their invasion, permanent writing media like clay tablets were not in common use in that area, and any writing they did have on papyrus would have perished. We do not know their language. As part of a mixed host they would have quickly taken up a language that was already established in their area, Canaanite. There is no real evidence as to what the Philistines' original language was. We have a couple of names, Goliath being one, which are probably Philistine in origin. We would consider them to be a crude and brutal people, living by the sword.

Compared to the Israelites, however, the Philistines were not crude at all. Their material culture was much more elegant than that of the Israelites. They decorated their pottery with pictures of birds that are virtually indistinguishable from the pottery decorations that were then in vogue on the Greek mainland, so that an archaeologist would be hard pressed to determine whether a given potsherd was Greek or Philistine unless he had a clue as to where it was found (or unless he had the chemistry of the clay analyzed). Their lifestyle included the crude luxuries of a previously settled people, not like the simple lifestyle of the previously nomadic Israelites or even of the Canaanites, and much of their everyday objects had a decorative component. They probably smelled better than the Israelites.

So when we call someone who is uncultured or unappreciative of art "a Philistine," we are faulting the wrong people.

The very few remains of their temples hint at the structure of palatial buildings in Greece of the immediately previous time. A central hearth-like circle, with roof-supporting columns beside it, appears to be shown in some ruins.

The Bible states that they came from Caphtor, or Crete. This is possible, especially since we know that Crete was at that time the fiefdom of the Mycenaean Greeks. To some archaeologists there is evidence of their having passed through Cyprus. But unlike the other Sea Peoples, we don't even have a good likelihood that we finally know the true ethnic identity of the Philistines.

Now, a sidelight that is actually close to the center of what was happening. About the time that the Sea Peoples began to move, a tribe, probably in the northern part of what is now Turkey, discovered a way to more easily refine iron.

Up until then iron was rare, although iron ore is found all over the world. It is probable that some of the iron that was in use had been reclaimed from iron meteorites. But iron had been made from the abundant ore for centuries, though in such small amounts as to not be profitable. Smelting iron requires much higher temperature than does smelting copper, and reliable ways to do it were hard to develop.

At any rate iron was worth several times its weight in gold. The "Bonze Age" is called that for a reason. Until iron became common, the most useful and practical metal was bronze, an alloy of copper and tin and sometimes arsenical copper. The international economy of the Bronze Age was tied to the trade in bronze raw material and especially in tin. Copper was found in good quantity in the Sinai and on the island of Cyprus though the supplies were running low by 1200 BC. Tin was harder to find, and as the Times of the Judges began, the major source of tin was southeast of the Black Sea near the present country of Georgia. Worse than shortage of tin at the sources, trade routes were closing due to the upheaval of populations.

Even bronze was not cheap. One reason elite warriors dominated warfare of that age is that only the elite could afford so much bronze as to make weapons. This, in turn, shaped the sociology of the times, in that the non-elite of any nation were not of as much account as were the leaders, and society was pretty hierarchical.

Sometime around 1300 to 1200 BC tribes just south of the tin deposits in the Caucasus had developed the economical production of iron in useful quantities. The Hittites had hegemony over this region, and they adopted iron making and kept the technology secret. Then the Hittites fell to the surge of Sea Peoples, particularly to the Luvians and Phrygians. The technology was now available to the Sea Peoples.

The impact of iron on social structure seems to have been radical. Iron ore is almost limitless, and once a way had been found to produce iron "easily" it became possible for the non-elite to be armed. Some historians credit the wide availability of iron for the social upheavals that came about at that time.

In their passage through and south of what is now Turkey the Sea Peoples picked up iron technology. As is usual for such things, the adoption of this technology was not instantaneous. The Sea Peoples continued to use bronze. A good example is the bronze spearhead of Goliath. However, it is clear that in time the Sea Peoples began to use iron, and it appears that they tried to keep it as their monopoly. They forbade the Israelites to have ironsmiths, and they charged a fee to do the ironwork that Israelite farmers needed for their plows and other tools (First Samuel 13:20). This prohibition must have held a few years after the invasion of the Sea Peoples in order for enough time to elapse for the Philistines to establish that much dominance over Israel.

On the other hand, it is likely that the Philistines had some use of iron at the time of the invasion, and that this technical superiority had some effect in their success.

This, then, was the invasion and its aftermath that dominates the second half of the Book of Judges and the first part of the Book of First Samuel, a time I have here designated as Phase Three of the process of Israel's occupation of the Land.

During this phase Israel is never said to have conclusively won against the Philistines, because even after the battles in which Israel won, the Philistines were still there and were still a thorn in Israel's side.

I mentioned that Rameses III of Egypt halted the Sea Peoples' advance in 1191 BC. He then did what his ancestor Rameses II had done with the early Sherden; he inducted defeated Sea People warriors into his own army. This was a wise strategy, one followed many times in history. You do not disband the army of a warrior culture and then expect the warriors to peacefully become civilians. If Rameses III had simply turned back the Sea Peoples and left the surviving warriors unemployed, there would be continued and inconvenient raiding, if not of Egypt itself, then of the territories that Egypt claimed as its nominal fiefdom. This way, Rameses III satisfied the main aim of his opponents, namely the occupation of land, but he also augmented his army with seasoned soldiers without having to levy against his own people. It cost Rameses III nothing to let the Philistines subjugate the Canaanite residents of the sea plain and harass the Israelites. He had "domesticated" the warriors.

Egypt ceded to the Philistines the territory that we call the Gaza Strip and the seacoast north of it to where modern Tel Aviv now stands.

Two features of this concession are salient in the Book of Judges: the five fortified cities of the sea plain (Gaza,

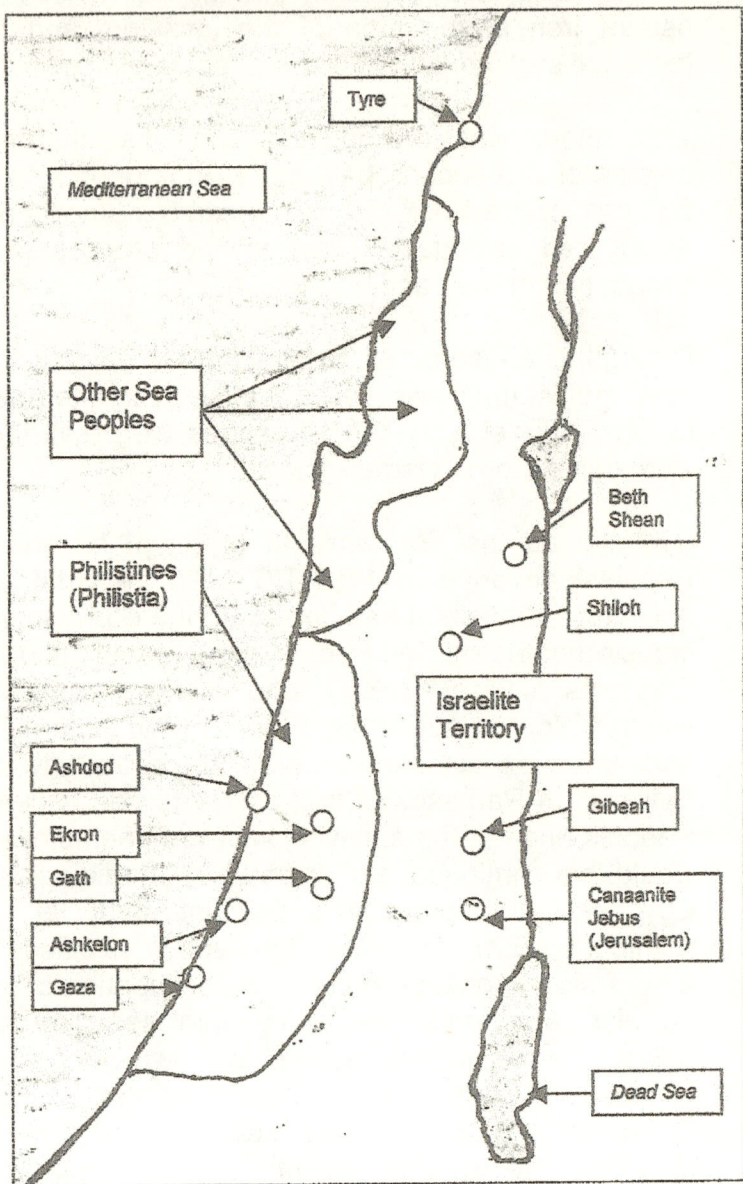

Fig. 8
Israel and Philistia after the settling in of the Sea Peoples, about 1100 BC.

Gath, Ashdod, Ekron and Ashkelon) became Philistine; and Philistine garrisons under Egyptian authority were stationed at key points in the Land (Beth Shean and Gibeah are mentioned, and there were no doubt others). These permanent thorns in Israel's side persisted until their final conquest by David. The garrison cities appear to have continued to be considered Canaanite city-states but with Philistine garrisons.

As to the other Sea Peoples, they settled onto other parts of the Levant. On the coast of Palestine the Philistines held the Gaza Strip and the land north as far as modern Tel Aviv. North of them the coast was held by the Sikels or Shiqalaya, as far at least as Dor, which is roughly modern Ceaserea. North of them, the coast including Acco was held by the Sherden or Shardana. We do not have definite locations for the other Sea Peoples, but it is likely that all of them became somewhat mixed. Like the Israelites, we will continue to call them all Philistines except when a distinction is helpful.

The settlement pattern that resulted is shown in Figure 8. Philistia was anchored by the five cities of the coastal plain. Other Sea Peoples were settled north of them, probably almost up to Tyre. The city of Tyre was independent, never having been conquered by the Sea Peoples.

The five cities of the coastal plain are frequently mentioned in the Book of Judges and in First Samuel. All this time, remember, the nation of Israel consisted of settlements. As the Book of Judges concludes, "There was no king [of Israel] in those days." The Israelite settlements were overlaid on a Canaanite land, with many remaining Canaanite settlements continuing to exist and with their inhabitants nominally subservient to Israel but practicing their old culture and religion. As best we can tell, the Philistines adopted some of the Canaanite culture and religion. So Israel settled into the Land in a matrix of hostile natives and invaders. Unlike Israel's enemies in the first and second phases, the invading Philistines were not camel-riding raiders, but settlers in their own right and might.

Several of the Judges in this phase are described as leading resistance to the Philistines.

Among the first of these would be Jephthah of Giliad (Judges 10:6 – 12:7) His opponents were both the Ammonites and the Philistines. We have no other reference for an alliance between those two peoples, and it doesn't have a counterpart in later developments. The Ammonites lived east of the Jordan Valley and the Philistines (actually in this case, the Sikels or the Sherdan) were on the Mediterranean coast, so their attack on Israel was a pincers that, as the Book says, "shattered Israel" and led to its domination by those enemies for 18 years.

Jephthah attacked the Ammorites and defeated them, destroying 20 towns. It may be significant that no record was made about any attack on the Philistines. From this we can infer that the alliance was not strong, and Ammon may have taken their supposed Philistine alliance too much for granted. It may also be that the Philistines were not yet fully established. At any rate, the enemies we find recorded from now on are the Philistines.

The story of Jephthah gives us an insight into the fact that the tribes of Israel were not fully unified. The evidence is indirect, but unmistakable: the tribes spoke different dialects of Hebrew. The men of the tribe of Ephraim could not pronounce the word "shibboleth." (Judges 12:5,6) We are again reminded that the Book of Judges ends with the statement, "There was no king in those days. Everyone did what was right in his own eyes."

The next three Judges in the record are not reported to have fought any external enemies. The Book of Judges says only that "after" Jephthah, a man named Ibzan of

74

Bethlehem in the tribal area of Zebulon was the Judge, and "after" him was Elon of Zebulon and that "after" him Abdon of Zebulon judged. These Judges are placed in Phase Three in this book by default, because we have no reason to doubt the "after" statement. In other cases, "after" seems to mean "sometime after that, but not necessarily right away" or "around that time." Precision in dating narratives is something that we Westerners are more concerned with than are other and older cultures.

These three Judges, then, were simply respected leaders whose authority was recognized to the extent that they were called Judges. It may be noteworthy that all three were from the tribe of Zebulon, whose allotment was in the valleys of the Kishon River and of Jezreel between the Sea of Galilee and Mt. Carmel. This is the area that is said elsewhere (Judges 1:30) to be one where the Canaanites were not fully driven out. It would also be the area where Philistines would most naturally go inland, since it is a well-traveled valley through which ancient trade routes led from the Mediterranean to the Jordan Valley and south to Arabia.

Saying that the Philistines were able to go inland from the area of modern area of Haifa is to use the same "lumping" name that the Israelites used – all Sea Peoples were Philistines. Actually, the Sea People who would have gone inland from this location would be Sikels or Sherdan. This has some bearing on the name of the general who commanded the Canaanite stronghold of Hazor (Sisera), his name being one that was used in the land that Sikels are presumed to come from, Sicily.

The story of the prophetess Deborah and her general Barak (Judges Chapters 4 and 5) must describe events that took place after the Sea Peoples invaded and long enough after the destruction of Hazor in about 1230 BC so that the city would have been re-occupied by the Canaanites. Hazor had been one of the greatest cities in the Levant before Joshua's conquest. Archaeology says that it did not get rebuilt to its former glory, but that there was a settlement that re-grew there. In the Deborah-Barak story, a king of Hazor called Jabin had oppressed the Israelites in that territory. Jabin was not a personal name. The king of Hazor whom Joshua defeated earlier also had the title of Jabin

Sisera was probably a Sikel mercenary in the service of this second Jabin. The Sikels held the seacoast just west of the location of Hazor, though Sisera lived at Harosheth ha Goyim (Smithy of the Gentiles) closer to the coast and next to the Kishon River. The use of Sea People mercenaries had been initiated by Egypt. The Canaanites also, it appears, had reached accommodation with the Sea Peoples. In this instance Jabin was able to command Canaanites over a wide area, and he had placed at Sisera's command a force of 900 chariots and presumably a comparable number of soldiers. This was a formidable army, which Barak defeated by shrewd strategy, entangling the chariots in the boggy terrain of the Kishon. The Book of Judges says that the Kishon swept them away in a flood, and an actual flood is also a possibility. The chariots of the day were a tremendous military force, but they were vulnerable to bogs, rocks and hills. And to shrewd military counter-tactics, such as enticing them into boggy ground and attacking them from their right, a direction to which archers cannot easily shoot and which is opposite from the shield arm. At least, such is the strategy I imagine in my fiction, without any warrant!

The Philistines who were establishing themselves at this time seem not to have been very interested in the hill country where most of Israel lived. Just as the Israelites had come to accommodation with the surviving Canaanites, so they seem to have adjusted to the Philistine settlements. Soon enough, the Philistines discovered the hills as a source of loot and they were aided by the fact that Egypt had located Philistine garrisons in some of the inland Canaanite cities such as Beth Shean and Gibeah or Gibeon. Then the Philistines rode rough-shod over Israel, "oppressing" Israel as the Book says.

The next Judge in the Book (Samson, Judges 13 – 16) is an illustration of the adjustment that had been reached between Israelite and Philistine neighbors. Archaeologists have found that Samson's hometown shows both Israelite and Philistine artifacts at this time. In other words, the two peoples were living mixed in the town. This may well have been true in other border locations. Kings may fight, but neighbors find ways to get along.

Samson was a man of the tribe of Dan though he was living in an area that had been allotted to the tribe of Judah. You will recall that the tribe of Dan had been ousted from its allotment around what is now Tel Aviv, and most of the tribe had moved to the area north of Israel's main allotments. Some Danites, such as Samson's ancestors, seem to have moved south into the territory of Judah.

Samson was a mighty adversary to the Philistines of the coastal plain. However, there is little indication that he was a leader of Israel. A hero, yes, but not a leader. His battles were personal, to avenge himself against insults and injuries. Even his status as hero to the Israelites is in doubt. When he hid from the Philistines after one of his escapades, the men of the tribe of Judah had no hesitation in turning him over to the Philistines.

As the Judahites did so, they made an illuminating comment. "Don't you know that the Philistines are rulers over us?" So we see that by Samson's time, the Israelites had ceded military dominance to the Philistines. This is the time when the Philistines were able to forbid Israel to have iron-smiths. The monopoly on iron was too valuable to let the hill barbarians, as the Philistines no doubt considered Israelites to be, to have iron technology. Clearly, Philistia was in control of at least part of the

Israelite hill country, and perhaps their control extended to part of the Jordan Valley. Certain it is that they had a Jordan Valley foothold with their garrison at Beth Shean adjacent to the upper Jordan Valley.

We should not expect that the Philistines were a single nation under a single king. There were five dominant Philistine cities, plus the garrisons. All our surviving records indicate that the cities were like Greek city-states, each commanding its surrounding farms and villages and each seeking its own advantage. Yet there was cooperation among the city-states, and as always there were the ties of blood and culture, among the Philistines as well as among the Israelites and Canaanites.

Neither should we expect that the Philistine garrisons in the Land were under the firm control of Egypt. Egypt had continued to decline after its desperate and successful defense against the Sea People invasion. Its settlement with the Sea Peoples indicates that it had not crushed them (though of course the Pharaoh's scribes claimed that) and instead had to give them places to live. It was no problem to the Egyptians that the place to live was at the expense of the Canaanites of the coastal plain. After the garrisons were settled inland, Egypt appears to have largely let them be self-supporting. We do not have records of Egypt collecting taxes from the Land, for example.

Phase Three thus ends with the three peoples – Philistines, Canaanites, and Israelites – having come to some kind of accommodation. The accommodation was unequal and unstable. But the Israelites had dominance in the hill country and across the Jordan. Canaanites were scattered among the Israelites, in varying degrees of subservience and with some fully independent strong points such as Jerusalem. The Philistines were centered on five fortress city-states and in garrisons as far as the center of the Land, and Israel was subservient to them.

On the coastal plain itself it is probable that much of the population was Canaanite, dominated by Philistines.

The Hittite Empire was no more, and Egypt was too weak to have any real effect in the Land.

The Land's instability manifested itself in continuing Philistine incursions into what it regarded as its vassal territory, Israel. This would come to a head in our Phase Four.

Fourth Phase: Establishing a Kingdom

The fourth phase is dominated by the overpowering personality of Samuel, the last Judge and the first Prophet. This includes not only the story of Samuel, the last Judge and the first Prophet, but also the stories of Kings Saul and David. (The last-mentioned is so famous that his early life and anointing will not be recounted here. The reader is referred to Chapters 16-27 in the Book of First Samuel.)

The first part of Samuel's story carries no hint of Philistine oppression. His early life seems to have taken place in a sort of Shangri La, the Sanctuary at Shiloh. The picture we can get of Shiloh is revealing of the situation *vis a vis* the Philistines, in part in an argument from silence.

The Israelites had a nation-wide Sanctuary at Shiloh in the hill country in the middle of the Land. The city sat just over the western crest of the steep slope upward from the Jordan Valley. The Philistines did not interfere with it, and all of Israel was able to come individually to the Sanctuary. At the Sanctuary the High Priest conducted the ceremonies that were required of both individual Israelites and of the nation as a whole.

The sum of what we can gather from various sources is that the Philistines were quite tolerant of religions. From analogy to the homelands of the Sea Peoples we infer that they respected the practices of all religions. They adopted local religions, though we find no indication that they adopted any part of the worship of the LORD. The exclusiveness of the Israelite religion militated against its being adopted by outsiders.

The Philistines were by this time an accepted presence in the Land. They were, in a sense, a reliable thorn in Israel's side; they lorded it over the Israelites but things were stabilized. The Philistines' role was that of an occupying army, spread thin in scattered garrisons except on the Mediterranean plain where they had their five great cities. The Israelite Sanctuary at Shiloh did not hold portable wealth of the kind that would tempt raiders. The sheep and other sacrificial animals that the Israelites brought to the Sanctuary were of no great use to the Philistines.

As to the small amount of gold and the few jewels in the Sanctuary furniture and in the High Priest's vestments, they were temple property, and it seems that Philistines honored the religions of the people they lived among. I wonder if the experience of the Achaeans in their theft of a priest's daughter (see the opening chapter of the *Iliad*) and the disaster it brought on the Achaean host was a remembered element in the Philistines' culture. There was a reverence for others' religious property behind the Philistines' later treatment of the Ark of the Covenant (First Samuel 4 – 6).

So, although the Philistines dominated Israel to the extent of forbidding the practice of iron-smithing, the Sanctuary at Shiloh was left out of the Israelite-Philistine conflict during Samuel's early years.

Samuel was dedicated by his parents to the service of the LORD at Shiloh. All sorts of theological issues are raised by how Samuel's service was carried out, though these issues are beyond the scope of this book. With regard to the social and military and political picture of the day, we do get some hints from Samuel's story.

Samuel's childhood life probably overlapped with the life of Samson. The accommodation of the Israelites to the Philistines held steady and Samson's personal exploits did nothing to upset it. Pressures were building, however.

When Samuel was a young man the Israelites gathered to fight the Philistines *en masse*. The date was probably between 1075 BC and 1050 BC.

The outcome of the Israelite revolt could have been predicted. A mass of untrained farmers and city burgers, lacking iron weapons and probably short of bronze weapons as well, went out to fight an organized army of trained soldiers. They were crushed.

First Samuel Chapter 4 tells us that the Israelites then called for the Ark of the Covenant to be brought to their camp to ensure that the LORD would fight for them.

Regardless of what one may think of the theological issue here, what happened next is consistent with what we know and surmise about the Philistines. To see the Israelites' potent religious symbol, the Ark, would give them pause. They, like all the people of that day, had a reverence for the god of the land, whoever he was. And the Ark had figured so prominently in the takeover of Canaan by the Israelites that the Philistines would rightly fear it. It is also consistent with military logic that the Philistines would exhort each other to fight for their lives when faced by the Ark, as the Book records.

Bringing the Ark did not save Israel. Thousands were killed. The Philistines captured the Ark. The Book of First Samuel relates how they treated the Ark with honor, housing it in the temple of their god Dagon and handing it off like a hot potato among their cities as plagues came upon them.

There is something about that plague that still puzzles those who try to understand it. The most plausible explanation is that it was the bubonic plague. The evidence is partly in the symptoms and partly in the response the Philistines made to it and partly in what sometimes happens to a people who move into a region and who are not familiar with the local practices by which the established people protected their health.

The symptoms certainly fit the bubonic plague, with the "tumors" or buboes. Then Dagon, in whose temple the

Ark had been housed, was a god of the grain and grain attracts rats. The Philistines made golden rats or mice as an offering to the God whom they had offended, indicating some connection there. Finally, a grain-raising people like the Canaanites had probably found that they had to avoid sick rats, or even that they had to protect their grain so as not to attract rats, in order to keep their health. A more recent and more explicit example is that of the hunters of marmot pelts who moved into Manchuria in the early 20th Century and who didn't observe the local taboo on handling sick rodents, and they touched off an epidemic of bubonic plague. And it must be remembered that the Philistines were Sea Peoples who traded widely in ships, and ships transport rats. All this may be coincidence, in view of the fact that it has not been shown by other sources that plague existed in Canaan before the 13th Century AD.

The Philistines and the Israelites attributed all this to the LORD. Many who believe in the Bible contend that this is how the LORD worked, whether or not He used a plague or created a new and miraculous affliction.

Every indication we have is that the Israelite-Philistine accommodation continued. However, though the Philistines returned the Ark to Israel, the Sanctuary at Shiloh ceased to be the rallying point of Israel. Archaeology verifies that it was destroyed. The Philistines probably did not touch the Sanctuary. But Shiloh without the Ark and without a High Priest was no longer the center of Israelite community life. It ceased to be a city about this time, and it remains in ruin.

The battle with the Philistines at Aphek with the loss of the Ark just before the death of Eli the High Priest is shown in Figure 9, together with additional clashes with the Philistines under Samuel and Saul.

(As a side comment, we may reiterate that Egypt at this time was no longer the dominant player in the region. It was a much-reduced empire under a line of weak Pharaohs. It left the Philistines as the autonomous occupiers of the Gaza Strip and the interior of the Land, with the other Sea Peoples holding the northern coast of the Land in similar independence. The Phoenician cities of Tyre and Sidon seem never to have been conquered by the Sea Peoples and they remained in the hands of Canaanites, though we now call them Phoenicians. Israel and Philistia were left to settle their relationship on their own, and the Philistines continued to dominate Israel.)

Up to this point, there is nothing to show that anyone was going about to establish a Kingdom of Israel.

The furniture of the Sanctuary other than the Ark must have been taken somewhere and preserved after the battle of Aphek. We next learn of a priestly establishment much later at Nob, near Jerusalem. The records of the Israelite High Priest succession are questionable during this period.

Though we have no direct evidence, I think that it is likely that the priests at Shiloh had kept a record of events similar to the *Anglo Saxon Chronicle*. This, in addition to oral tradition, would be the source of the history of Israel. Bear in mind that Israel was a literate society – the Judge Gideon "caught a young man of Succoth in the field," a young man at random, and had him write down the names of his city elders. The Canaanites and Israelites had an alphabet, and with an alphabet almost anyone can learn to read and write. Certainly the priest could do so. And the urge to preserve records is universal among literate people. So I think that we can assume that there were records at Shiloh that were, like the Sanctuary furniture, taken away and preserved. They would be the source of some of the Biblical record.

Out of this emerges Samuel, the man who was the main instrument in the creation of a nation called Israel.

Samuel is an enigma. This is a man who was first an assistant to the High Priest, then recognized as a leader, a seer and a Judge, then a man who disappeared into a family for some years, who then again emerged as the one Judge of the Israelites and acting High Priest, then as a war leader, and then as the one who anointed not one, but two, kings. He is at the center of Phase Four, the making of a kingdom.

We have two contradicting accounts of his ancestry. The account in First Samuel gives his tribal identity as Ephraimite. The later-written Book of First Chronicles (6:25-28) gives his tribal identity as Levite. It is likely that Samuel himself wrote at least the draft of First Samuel, as well as all of Judges, though it may have been extensively edited later. The motivation of an editor of First Samuel would be to reconcile the later actions of Samuel (he acted as High Priest) with his ancestry, so it would have taken conscientious fidelity to the story for him to keep Samuel's Ephraimite identity. The First Chronicles account is clearly intended to show the legitimacy of succession of the individuals who returned to Judah from the Babylonian captivity. The motivation of any editor of First Chronicles would be to show prestigious Levite ancestry for the individuals who claimed descent from Samuel's family. My opinion, therefore, is that Samuel was of the tribe of Ephraim and was not a Levite, much less of the priestly line in Levi. This makes his actions all the more remarkable.

After the Philistines returned the Ark to Israel, twenty years of stalemate ensued. During all this time, we may imagine, the Israelites chafed under Philistine domination. Most likely the surviving Canaanites did, too.

Israel as a nation seems to have shut down. All that remained of unity, now that the Sanctuary was inoperable, was the Judgeship of Samuel. He lived at his ancestral home at Ramah, a town in the tribal area of Ephraim in the center of the hill country. He had been recognized as a seer while he still lived at Shiloh and while the High Priest Eli was alive. Now he was the only rallying point for the Israelites, and his Judgeship probably began small and was enlarged as his fame grew. He was doing nothing then to establish a kingdom; he was only mediating disputes and when appropriate giving prophetic advice.

We can only imagine how Samuel went about unifying Israel. We are told that he established a circuit among the leading towns, operating as a traveling courtroom. At some point, and maybe from the beginning, he was offering sacrifices for the people.

The Biblical record and archaeology agree that, during this time, Israelites conducted worship of the LORD on "high places" throughout the Land. At least some of the worship contained elements of the old Canaanite religion. For example, the figure of a bull has been found in a hilltop shrine that was most likely Israelite. It is probable that the worshippers considered the Canaanite elements to be appropriate to the worship of the LORD. The high places themselves had often been the sites of Canaanite worship, in the manner that high places have been worship sites throughout the world.

It is not likely that Samuel would approve of Asherah poles, but there are recorded instances where he did lead worship on "high places." These were hillocks where it was natural to establish a place of worship. Though the Law as given to Moses was against it, this practice is nearly universal. People will worship their God, even when the official site is no longer available. Shiloh was gone, the Sanctuary was dispersed, and while the returned Ark had a Levite-custodian appointed by the local population, there was no Israel-wide location for worship. Solomon's Temple was a hundred years in the future. And when that Temple was destroyed, the Jews in Babylon invented the synagogue as a place to meet. When the Romans destroyed the later Herod's Temple

1100 years after Samuel, the synagogues dispersed throughout the world. It's a durable pattern.

The difference in Samuel's day from the later synagogue movement was that the Israelites were worshipping on what had been pagan sites, and some were mixing pagan elements into their worship. A synagogue is a place of study and teaching, not of worship *per se*, and certainly not a place for an altar of sacrifice.

In this gap there was only Samuel. The Philistines, as was their apparent practice, let him alone.

Samuel acceded to the role of priest and later as High Priest in offering sacrifices for the whole nation. This is the Samuel conundrum. Even if he were a Levite, which I doubt, that would not authorize him to offer sacrifices and certainly would not authorize him to offer sacrifices on behalf of the nation. Still, the record that he did these things is credible.

Meanwhile, Egypt had deteriorated further and had become even less of a factor in the Levant. In the middle of the Times of the Judges Rameses the Third had stopped the Philistines at Egypt's borders and he continued to rule with some success at first. But things fell apart. There was an economic bust, during which an unprecedented thing happened – workmen carried out a strike over unpaid wages. The workers complained, "We are starving hungry ... We are lacking oil. We have no fish, not even vegetables." Finally there was a plot, implicating the harem, to assassinate Rameses III. It may have succeeded, though all we know of that is that he died during the time of the trials of the assassins. Perhaps he died as the delayed result of the assassination.

After Rameses III died a line of Pharaohs who also carried the name of Rameses but who became successively weaker ruled Egypt. These rulers left little by the way of monuments. Egypt was invaded by Libya to its west and then by Nubia to its south. We have to conclude that this impotency of Egypt had to figure in the opportunity for Israel to form a kingdom.

Egypt broke into two kingdoms: one ruled by Pharaohs of the 21st Dynasty and the other by the priests and generals. The more vigorous and unified Egypt of the 22nd Dynasty had not yet come into its own after the Libyan take-over of the Pharonic line.

Egypt of that time left some written records, but not about Israel. Israel's former neighbors to the north, the literate Hittites, had been destroyed in the Sea Peoples turmoil and their writing system had been forgotten. The literate Kassites still ruling in Mesopotamia were not interested in the Land. The apparently non-literate Philistines have left us no writings at all. The only record of events in Israel we have of these years is the Book of First Samuel, and it is stingy with its information. We have to read between the lines.

Another Israelite revolt against the Philistines was inevitable. Preparation took twenty years, while Samuel led the Israelites in a revival of the Law.

It appears that Samuel took over some kind of leadership after the loss of the Israelite center at the Sanctuary of Shiloh. He had already made a reputation as one who could consult the LORD, under conditions where men from all the tribes could see his status while he was still at Shiloh and remember that status after the loss and recovery of the Ark. Filling in a blank, I think that he gradually built a traveling courtroom and became the Judge of all the tribes. When he was old, it is recorded, he maintained a circuit among a limited number of cities. We can reasonably assume that this limited number reflects a constriction from an Israel-wide circuit of some sort that he established when he was young. It is also reasonable to assume that the practice of going to consult him, established while he was still at Shiloh, continued when he moved to his ancestral home at Ramah.

Most likely Samuel did not conduct his Judgeship with the intent of organizing the revolt against the Philistines. Rather, he led a concerted drive to bring Israel into return to the Law and the worship of the LORD. This "seeking of the LORD" by Israel is the substance of what record was left to us in the Book of First Samuel about those years. "So Israel put away their Baals and Ashtoreths and served the LORD only." (First Samuel 7:4)

Then Samuel called for an all-Israel conference at Mizpah. This town was about 7 miles north of what is now Jerusalem, in the hill country of Benjamin. The Philistines took note.

Picture the situation from the Philistine point of view. They held the coastal plain, in five fortified cities, where they had ruled unopposed for about a century. They had garrisons scattered over the Israelite territory. The Israelites were subject to them, and it is likely that they considered the whole Land to be theirs and that the Israelites were simply a major people who lived in their land. One of their garrisons was at Gibeah, the large Benjamite town less than five miles from the Israelite assembly at Mizpah.

The Israelites were called together for religious purposes, according to Samuel's call, but the Philistines surely smelled rebellion. One of the most effective tactics of control over people is to forbid assembly, and now the Israelites were assembling in some very large number.

The Philistines must have been informed of the assembly well before it took place. This gave them time to mount a punitive expedition. Crushing this incipent revolt must have looked easy to Philistia. They had troops and chariots enough to take any city and to defeat any force that these hill barbarians could put together, lacking as the Israelites were in iron weapons. The Philistines were disciplined warriors moving against a mob. It was to be a massive but easy punitive expedition.

The record in First Samuel implies that the Philistine advance was not anticipated by Israel. But Samuel would have had to be blind to the obvious not to have known what would result if he called an assembly, and all indications are that he was a very astute man. The other Israelite leaders may not have known, but Samuel certainly did. It may have been his way to force a showdown. At any rate, a showdown was what he got.

Since the fall of Jericho 200 years earlier all the events of this history have been reasonably derived from the military and political and social situations. This next one is not. The writer of our only record makes no bones about the fact that what happened was the work of the LORD of Israel and His thunder.

First Samuel (Chapter 7) reports that, when the Philistines came against Mizpah and Samuel interceded with the LORD for Israel, "the LORD thundered with loud thunder against the Philistines and threw them into such a panic that they were routed before the Israelites."

Thunder, especially supernaturally loud thunder with an accompanying unseasonable storm, has always been seen by ancient peoples as the voice of a god. It is also is sure to induce panic in horses, and the Philistines may have been arrogant enough to bring their chariots into the hill country. Chariots are well enough on the plain, and even in the hill country if you are taking one or two or even a column along a beaten path, but the hill country is no place for a chariot charge or retreat. Once panic sets in and horses are plunging about and upsetting chariots, even disciplined troops can be broken up. The Philistines broke in panic. Then the Israelites charged.

The wild rush of Israelites energized by their confidence in Samuel's intercession with the LORD and enraged by years of Philistine oppression, even if they were simply a charging mob, is not something that can be easily withstood by troops that are already disorganized. The Israelites may not have had technically advanced iron weapons but hoes and sickles and axes and even clubs can be effective, not to mention the dropped Philistine weapons that would have been snatched up. And we must not forget that the Philistines were, on other evidence, afraid of the LORD of Israel. Yes, it is reasonable to believe the report of Chapter 7. The Philistines were routed and chased all the way down to the plain.

This battle seems to have changed the relationship between Philistia and Israel for a while. The five Philistine cities of the plain were secure, as was the hold of the Philistines on the plain itself. But their control over upland Israel was apparently no longer complete. They were still the enemy of Israel, they could still forbid the working of iron by Israelites, and they still had a garrison in at least one fortified city, Beth Shean. We recall that garrison when we read of what happened to the body of King Saul (First Samuel 31:10) some 50 years later. But they did not invade Israel in full force for half a century.

On the other hand, the Philistine presence had also provided some protection from other Israelite enemies, those to the east. Evidence of this is also in the future, but only by less than 10 years.

Another result was that the Israelites saw the power that they had been given, and they pressed Samuel to give them a king so that they could be like other nations, with a king to lead them in battle. Samuel at first hesitated and waited until he had prayed to the LORD. Then, assured that the LORD approved the move and setting aside his personal resentment, Samuel agreed. He warned the people about what a king would be like, a warning that events later fulfilled.

This demand for a king had been foreseen in the time of Moses over 200 years earlier, who expounded the Law and said, among many other things, "When you enter the land the LORD your God is giving you and you have taken possession of it and settled in it, and you say, 'Let us set a king over us like the nations around us...'" The people of Israel evidently thought that now they had indeed settled the Land. More to the point, they had had a bad experience with the system of Judges.

Samuel had been a mighty hero to them. Now he was old. He had attempted to install his sons as deputies but it was a disaster. His sons corrupted the law. The Judgeship lost its credibility with the people.

First Samuel Chapters 9 and 10 tell of how the king was selected and announced. Samuel anointed Saul, the son of Kish of Gibeah in Benjamin, as king. Then both Saul and Samuel went to their homes.

The Philistines were less in control of the Land, and outsiders saw an opportunity. The Ammonites, a people who had been engulfed by Israel in the initial conquest, fired the opening shot. They were a smaller group than some of Israel's neighbors and their aggression was correspondingly small. They besieged a single city in Gilead, on the east side of the Jordan River, in the territory that had been allocated to the Israelite tribe of Gad.

The full story will not be repeated here. I recommend that you read Chapter 11 in the Book of First Samuel. Briefly, the Ammonites demanded that the residents of Jabesh of Gilead accept either total massacre or surrender and have their right eyes gouged out. This gives us a picture of the nature of warfare in those days, when there was no Geneva Convention.

Israel's King Saul, a simple farmer until now, issued a call for the Israelites to join him and rescue the besieged city. He bade them to assemble or have their oxen cut in pieces – a threat that, picturesque and illustrated with the pieces of his own oxen, was effective. The Israelite army of 30,000 raised the siege of Jabesh and destroyed the Ammonite army. Israel suddenly recognized that they had a king. The nation had been officially formed.

Samuel made his retirement speech. He called down a terrific rainstorm in a month when it never rains in the Land to show that the LORD was displeased with the change from a loose theocracy under a Judge to a regular kingdom with a secular ruler. The assembled Israelites cowered under the storm and Samuel reassured them while admonishing them to remain faithful to the LORD.

The last of the Judges had ceased to judge. Now there was a king, and he would be responsible for justice in the Land. But Samuel was still the prophet and his work was not yet done.

Samuel also continued to serve as *de facto* High Priest of Israel. The next episode in the Book of First Samuel (remember that there is little or no information about this period of time in the Land except for the Bible) has the son of King Saul, Jonathan, stirring up a hornet's nest by attacking the Philistine outpost at Geba in the hill country north of Saul's home at Gibeah. This bit of information tells us that the Philistines still had garrisons in Israelite territory, even though they did not have the same total control that they had before their defeat under Samuel. "And the Philistines heard of it," as the Bible says. Of course. Now the fat was in the fire.

Saul sent out the news also among the Israelites, warning them that his new kingdom had "become a stench to the Philistines" and summoning the Israelite warriors to meet with him at Gilgal, the old camp of Joshua after the

Exodus. But when the Philistines mustered an army led by 3,000 chariots, the Israelites hid in fear.

Samuel had agreed to meet Saul at Gilgal. He delayed and Saul became impatient. He did what Samuel was supposed to do – to offer, like a High Priest, a sacrifice on behalf of Israel. Samuel arrived as Saul was finishing and he broke down in sorrow and rage. Saul had blasphemed by trying to go beyond his secular kingly role and taking on the role of a priest. Samuel pronounced the doom of Saul's line and went home, leaving Saul and Israel to their fate.

Matters hung in the balance. Then Saul's son Jonathan took the fight to the Philistines in accordance with Philistine custom. He went as single champion to the Philistine outpost and successfully cut his way through their forces. The rest of Israel, encouraged by his feat, rallied out of hiding. You may recall that the Philistines respected the single champion, whether like Achilles in the Iliad or like Goliath (later) calling out David (First Samuel 17). Goliath would, in fact, declare that whoever prevailed in single combat would give victory to his side. So Jonathan's feat signaled, at least culturally if not in reality, that the Philistines were defeated. Panic set into the Philistine army again, and they were melting away.

King Saul first decided to consult the LORD before attacking the Philistines, then in the urgency of joining battle he recalled the consultation. He attacked, and found that the Philistines were not only fearful but were also self-destructive. There is a revealing sentence in the record: "Those Hebrews who were previously with the Philistines and had gone up with them to their camp went over to the Israelites and were with Saul and Jonathan" (First Samuel 14:21). This obscure sentence reveals how much the Israelites (Hebrews) and the Philistines had accommodated to each other, and it calls to mind the (later) episode of David volunteering to join a Philistine army. Clearly, there was at least a zone, probably in the

95

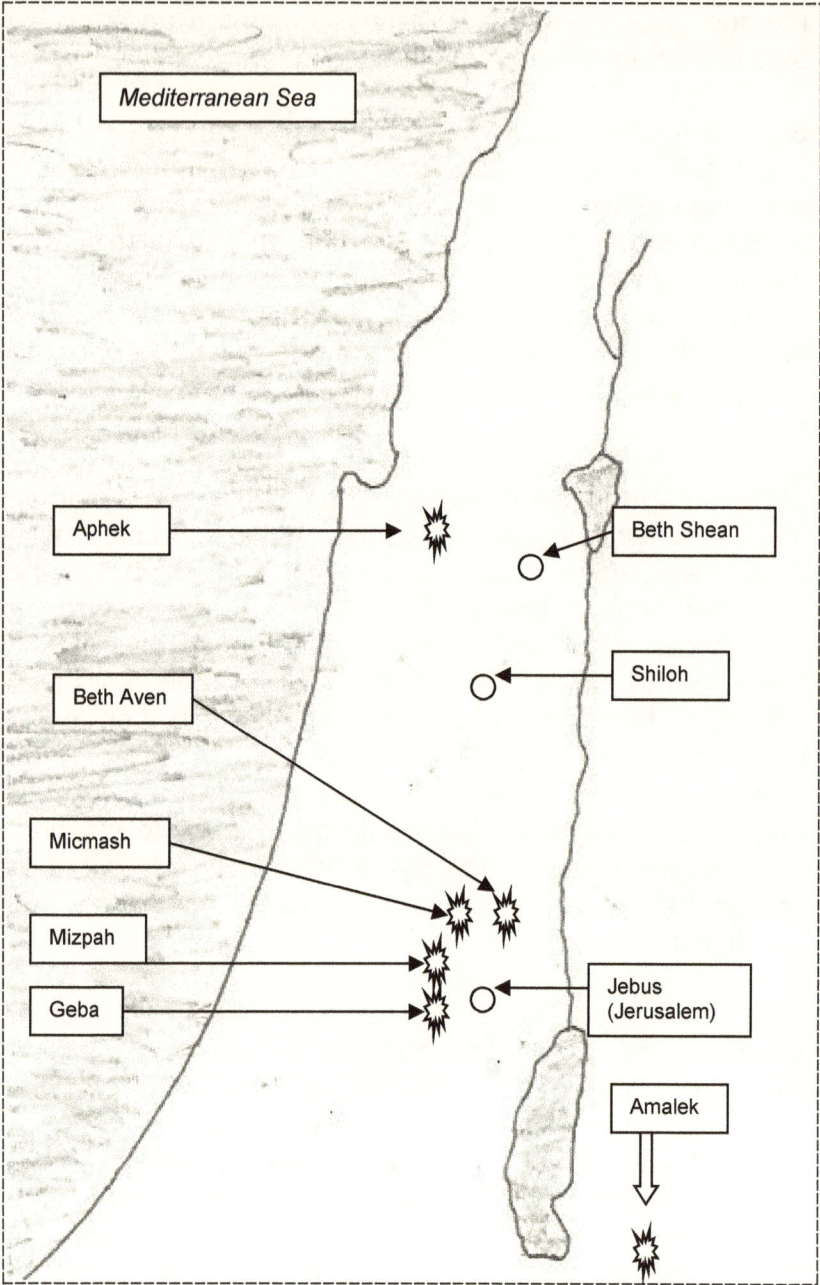

Mediterranean Sea

Aphek

Beth Shean

Shiloh

Beth Aven

Micmash

Mizpah

Geba

Jebus
(Jerusalem)

Amalek

**Fig. 9
Clashes with the Philistines
under Eli, Samuel, and Saul**

western foothills, where the two peoples lived together as one Philistine nation.

The new kingdom of Israel was still straightening out what a secular kingdom means. The Philistines were defeated and the victorious but exhausted Israelites "fell upon the plunder." They started to slaughter cattle to eat, and did it urgently, without properly draining the blood. Saul – Saul, the secular king! – stopped them and instructed them to do the slaughter in the kosher manner. Then Saul turned to the matter of whether to pursue the defeated Philistines onto the plain. He called a priest and inquired of the LORD for direction. At this juncture, when it should have been clear that the only course of action was to hit the Philistines hard while they were in retreat, this secular king who had always been so impulsive called for a priest.

There was no answer to whatever supplication was made. Then, as you will read in the story in the second half of Chapter 14, the whole matter dissolved in each side withdrawing to its own land. The status of the Israel-Philistia conflict reverted to what it had been before.

The record is that there was open warfare between Saul and the Philistines all the days of his kingship.

Samuel, then an old man, came to Saul and as a prophet announced that the LORD required a service of this king who had been amassing a standing army. Saul was to go against the Amalekites and destroy them utterly, sparing neither people nor cattle nor property. This was because the nomadic Amalekites had attacked Israel over 200 years earlier during the Exodus, and no doubt also because during the pre-Philistine days the Amalekites had raided Israel.

Saul warned the Kenites, a group related to Israel and who had partially merged with Israel, to get out of the way, and he led his army south. The Israelite army failed to carry out the instructions completely. They did indeed kill people thoroughly, but they kept the best of the cattle and other loot, and took the king of the Amalekites captive. Samuel went to Saul in a towering rage on behalf of the LORD. He personally killed the Amalekite king and deposed Saul from the anointed kingship. Then Samuel went home.

The new Israelite kingdom still had a king, Saul, but the Divine Right had been taken away. The officials about Saul no doubt rallied to support him since their own tenure depended upon his remaining king. The kingdom continued to function. However, it must have been a dispirited time for the new nation.

Samuel had one last task. He was commanded by the LORD to make another king. He went as instructed to the city of Bethlehem and anointed an unlikely young man, the youngest in the family of Jesse, a youth who would become the famous King David. Samuel then went home for the last time. He had carried out his final obligation in the process of creating a nation.

Samuel died soon after, before David ascended to the throne. With the death of the last Judge, Samuel, the Times of the Judges came to a close.

After the Times of the Judges

Samuel left the incipient kingdom while Saul was still king. This was about the year 1018 BC. Samuel was about 77 years old when he died.

The new Israelite kingdom was strong enough to hold off the Philistines. The Philistines apparently controlled the coastal plain with their five cities and also the foothills. In the foothills, it seems, there was a mixed population of Philistines and Israelites. The hill country, the Jordan valley and the territory east of the Jordan were fairly securely in the hands of Israel except for the garrison city of Beth Shean. That city was Canaanite under Philistine control.

There may have been other Philistine garrison cities as well. The Philistine garrison that had been at Gibeah seems to have been expelled, because King Saul of Israel made Gibeah, his hometown, the capitol of his kingdom. What is probably his home and throne room have been excavated. Scratched on the floor is a game board. The building had no fine stonework and the place was fairly small. The court of Saul must have been a crude place compared to our usual picture of a palace. The king had attached to himself many men whom he had noted to be outstanding and who constituted his palace guard and the core of his standing army as well as his courtiers. We know of at least one source of court entertainment besides the floor game – Saul conscripted David as personal musician.

The war between Saul and the Philistines continued during all his reign. We are not given details such as locations or sizes of the battles. Neither side overpowered the other, and this was a new development. Before this the Philistines had been the clear overlords.

Outside the Israelite kingdom and the Philistine coast, the international situation was again such that outside empires did not interfere with the local fighting.

Egypt, as noted in the previous chapter, had broken apart in civil war and was two kingdoms. The northern Egyptian kingdom kept moving its capitol in response to the internal upheavals. The southern kingdom was naturally out of touch with the Levant and was ruled by a succession of rulers who were not Pharaohs. Power passed to the priesthood and, at least in theory, the real ruler was the god Amun with the priests ruling in his name. During the later lifetime of Samuel the king of northern Egypt was the founder of the 21st Dynasty, and he ruled for nearly 50 years. So Egypt in the north, the part that could have had any impact on the Levant, was stable but not strong enough to exert much influence on its neighbors. Not until 945 BC, well into the reign of David's son Solomon, was Egypt reunited into a single country with the strong founder of the 22nd Dynasty, Sheshonk, in control – but that is ahead of our story.

In the north of Israel, Assyria was quiescent. Its "empire" was in decline, assailed from the south by Aramaeans. Not until a hundred years later would Assyria re-emerge as an empire to be reckoned with. The Aramaeans who were pressing Assyria were the immediate northern neighbors of Israel, but for some reason they were not a threat to the emerging Israelite kingdom. The Syrian nation that David's successors struggled with was derived from the Aramaeans, but that was later.

To the west were the Philistines, of course, and beyond them was the Mediterranean Sea. During this time, and in fact ever since the Sea Peoples settled down, the sea was an ocean of only peaceful trading.

To Israel's east was the desert. Only nomadic tribes lived there, as well as to the south in the same desert where Saul had decimated the Amalekites.

Israel, apart from its ongoing conflict with the Philistines, was free to develop its kingdom.

A kingdom was a new thing for Israel to grapple with and its first steps were confused. Saul had simply gone home after being anointed. His subsequent actions were a mixture of impulsiveness, false starts and drawing back, and an evident fear of Samuel. It must have seemed to Saul that he was in over his head and at the same time was required to take action. His first kingly action, that of rallying Israel to rescue the city of Jabesh, was both immediate and effective. After that he became unreliable.

While Saul was still king and after he had ruled for many years, Samuel had anointed a replacement king in the person of David. This act must have been confusing to everyone who was involved, not the least to David himself.

By two means (his defeat of the Philistine champion Goliath and his skill at singing to the accompaniment of the harp) David was inserted into the court of Saul without revealing that he was to be Saul's successor. David became King Saul's son-in-law and a military leader. Saul became more and more paranoid and subject to impulsive violence.

That David was a threat to his crown became very clear to Saul because of the young man's popularity. David had to escape the court. He assembled his own band of freebooters and became a kind of Robin Hood. This was an even greater threat to Saul.

The story is both complicated and engaging, and the reader is advised to look at the account in First Samuel16 to Second Samuel 5. Here, only the highlights that are essential to this story and that illuminate the history of the area will be recounted.

David continued for some time as a fugitive with a growing band of followers and Saul tried to hunt him down.

Eventually David took refuge with the Philistines in the city of Gath, taking 600 of his men with him. This event would be incomprehensible if the Israelites and the Philistines were, as is so often supposed, black-and-white enemies. In fact, as we have seen before and as we see so clearly in this episode, there was a great deal of intermixing.

The next event reveals even more clearly the ambiguous relationship between individual Israelites and Philistines. The Philistines assembled a great force for a decisive battle with Saul and the Israelites, and David and his men were accepted into the Philistine army for the battle. But on the way some of the Philistine generals objected, on the grounds that David had been a prominent enemy of the Philistine nation, and David was sent back. Thus he did not have to take a stand for either side.

The Philistines assembled on the relatively level plain in the valley of Jezreel, the land between the Sea of Galilee and the Mediterranean coast just north of modern Haifa. The Sikels and Sherdan, another component of the Sea Peoples, occupied the seacoast here. However, by this time apparently all the Sea Peoples were considered to be Philistines, or the Philistines had absorbed the others. The choice of battlefield made good sense because there the chariots of the Philistines could be used to maximum effect.

Saul took the challenge and accepted the choice of battlefield. He mustered Israel just south of the valley, around Mount Gilboa. Then "When Saul saw the Philistine army he was afraid." Maybe he realized too late that he should have lured the Philistines into the hill country for the battle. At any rate, in his fear he consulted a medium or witch.

The encounter with the medium reveals another of those obscure customs that are touched on in the Times of the Judges. The medium was asked to bring back the ghost of Samuel for consultation, bringing him up from the ground. This use of a lustral pit to invoke spirits and earth gods has been attested in other sources, including archaeology. The invocation was successful. The spirit complained of being disturbed but answered Saul's question by telling him that his fate was sealed. Israel would be defeated and Saul and his sons would be killed.

Most generals would withdraw for a more favorable time and place after having received and believed such a prophecy. Saul did not. He must have been in the grip of a fatalistic depression. He died in the battle and Israel was scattered.

What happened to David after being sent back tells us that the raiding of nomadic peoples had not completely ceased. While he was gone the Amalekites raided his headquarters at Ziklag. Saul's massacre of Amalekites had not destroyed the whole nation. This is not surprising because the Amalekites were nomads, distributed over a wide area of what is now the northern Arabian Desert. They intruded into the southern desert of Israel, where David and his men had been raiding them. David pursued the Amalekites and recovered his people and his property.

After the defeat of Israel the Philistines occupied the towns that the Israelites had fled in fear. They still had their garrison at Beth Shean, and they fastened the bodies of Saul and his sons to the city wall.

The men of Jabesh, whom Saul had rescued from the Ammonites, came and took Saul's body for proper burning and burial. David had genuine feelings for Saul. He went into deep public mourning over Saul and composed one of the songs (psalms) for which he became famous, ending with "How are the mighty fallen!"

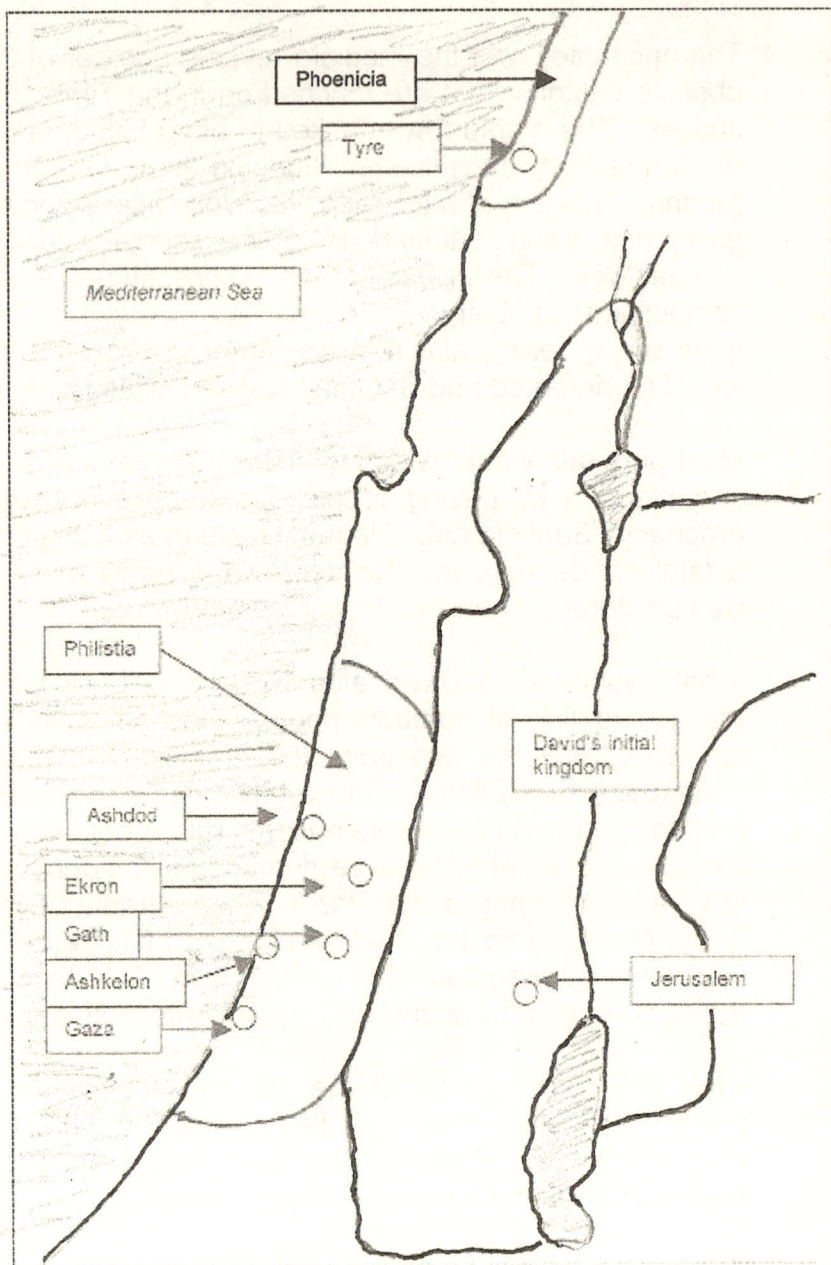

Phoenicia

Tyre

Mediterranean Sea

Philistia

Ashdod

Ekron

Gath

Ashkelon

Gaza

David's initial kingdom

Jerusalem

Fig. 10
David's initial kingdom
and Philistia

Then came the confused period that often follows the loss of both a king and a war. One Israelite faction went with Saul's surviving son and the smaller southern faction went with David. For some years David ruled his part of the Land from Hebron, south of Jerusalem. In a series of intrigues among generals, Saul's son was assassinated and David was proclaimed king over all Israel.

David's first move, showing his shrewdness as a politician, was to conquer Jerusalem. Recall that Israel had never been able to dislodge the Canaanites in Jebus, as the city was then called. But David needed a capitol that would be on neutral ground in order to heal the split between the north and south, and Jerusalem was just such a neutral spot, being on the north-south dividing line and with a secure hill fortress that had not previously belonged to either the north or the south faction.

David fought two major battles with the Philistines, reducing them to the status of subjects of Israel, though they continued to hold their cities and their coastal plain. The disposition of Israel and Phlilistia, with the new Phoenicia thrown in for good measure, is shown in Figure 10.

Thus we leave the post-Phase Four situation with the kingdom of Israel established. There was more to come, of course, including the reigns of David and of David's son Solomon. During Solomon's time, the Libyan Pharaoh Sheshonk of Egypt raided Jerusalem itself. But all those things are outside the scope of this book centered on the Times of the Judges.

APPENDIXES

Appendix A   Suggested Readings

Appendix B   The Peoples Mentioned in the Text

Appendix A:
Suggested Readings
for Broader Information

Though this book does not pretend to be scholarly and hence does not have a bibliography as such, there are some excellent sources for verifying and expanding its content. Only a few can be listed here to represent those that have contributed to the author's understanding over the past 75+ years of his interest in the stories. Some in this list are out of print because they are old, but they have not been surpassed in usefulness by younger sources I'm aware of. They might be found on Alibris.com or similar used-book listings.

The Books of **Judges and I Samuel** in **The Bible**. *A primary source for people and events.*

Biblical Archaeology Review, *a current periodical that sheds light on the ancient Middle East through contemporary archaeological reports.*

People of the Sea. *Trude Dothan and Moshe Dothan, 1992. Unsurpassed as a comprehensive account of the archaeological information that reconstructs the Philistines and other Sea Peoples.*

The Anglo-Saxon Chronicles, *a sort of year-by-year diary of England about 1000 years ago, mostly by monastic communities. It illustrates the kind of record that may have been kept by the priests of early Israel.*

The Anvil of Civilization. *Leonard Cottrell, 1957. Very readable coverage of the ancient Middle East.*

The Loom of History. *Herbert Miller, 1958. First chapters.*

The Secrets of the Hittites. *C. W. Ceram, 1973. Gives many quotations of records made by Middle Eastern peoples, including the Hittites and Egyptians, near and during the times of the Judges. See also Ceram's* Gods, Graves and Scholars.

History of the Jews. *Cecil Roth, 1961. First two chapters. Roth does not take the Joshua-Judges-Samuel account literally, but he summarizes his information and views well.*

Plagues and People, *William H. McNeill, 1976. Provides insight into the effects of movements of peoples.*

Guns, Germs and Steel, *Jared Diamond, 1999. Focus on the impact of technologies upon conflicts between peoples.*

The Penguin Atlas of Ancient History. *Penguin Books, 1967. Maps of the ancient world from earliest times to 362 AD. I am indebted to it for the locations of many of the peoples in this book's maps.*

And, for a "feel" for the Times, my own historical-fiction, pseudo-autobiographical books, **Judges, Rulers, and One Angry Levite**, *2007 and* **Samuel: Seer**, *2008, available from the author (see Title Page). This present book is intended to complete a trilogy with them.*

Appendix B:
The Peoples Mentioned in the Text

The many peoples who played a part in the Times of the Judges may be confusing. Their names are sometimes similar to each other and they may have variant spellings. Worse, some of them come to us from more than one language, so that what is intended to be the same name may sound quite different in the different languages. And then, of course, many of these foreign names sound peculiar to English-accustomed ears. This "people glossary" is intended to help with those problems.

Achaeans: *One of the Mycenaean Greek tribes who established a set of city-states in mainland Greece and probably on the western coast and islands of what is now Turkey long before the Times of the Judges. They dominated Crete in the 1300s BC and borrowed some of the more sophisticated Cretan civilization. Achaeans were the main Greek protagonists in the Trojan War. They were probably one of the Sea Peoples (see Ekwesh), arriving in the Land by way of Cyprus. Their material culture was similar to that of the Philistines.*

Ahiawasha: *Hittite name for a people who seem to have been the Achaeans.*

Amalekites: *A nomadic people who lived in northern Arabia and the Sinai, and who were camel-riding raiders in the time of Ehud and were organized into a more permanent or seasonal plundering body by the time of Gideon. King Saul and later David later waged a war of extermination against them. A southern remnant became part of the stock of the people we call Arabs.*

Ammonites: *A relatively small group of Canaanites or Aramaeans living east of the Jordan. They are not recorded as acting alone, probably because they were too small, until late in the Times of the Judges.*

Amorites: *A subset of Canaanites who lived along the Jordan River, with substantial power bases on the east of the river in the territories that were allotted to the tribes of Gad and Reuben.*

Aramaeans: *The Aramaeans were a numerous people living in what is now Syria and over into northern Iraq. They had been there for several centuries before the Times of the Judges. Some subdivisions of Aram had their own names as they emerged in some independence, such as the Assyrians. The Canaanites themselves can be considered a subset of Aramaeans. Very early in Israel's occupation of Canaan, they dominated much of Israel until the first Judge, Othniel, pushed them back. They formed the core of the peoples who show up much in later history as the Syrians (not the same as Assyrians).*

Assyrians: *This Semitic people lived north of the other Aramaeans, in the upper reaches of the Tigris and Euphrates rivers. During the Times of the Judges they were rebounding from their status as a minor buffer state and were asserting the expansionism that would mark them later as a warlike and highly aggressive state. At the Times of the Judges they were beginning to press on the Aramaeans south of them, who in turn pressed on Israel shortly after the time of Joshua.*

Canaanites: *A mixed people of West Semitic origin who lived in the land bearing their name, Canaan. Many of the other "...ites" mentioned in the Bible were subgroups of Canaanites. We usually call the northern Canaanites who survived into later times by the name of "Phoenicians."*

Denyen: *Egyptian name for what may well be the Homeric Greek Danoi. One of the Sea Peoples.*

Edomites: *A Semitic people who lived east and mostly south of the Dead Sea. During the Times of the Judges they were not recorded as hostile to Israel, though they had forced Moses to make a detour around their territory during the Exodus.*

Ekwesh: *Egyptian name for what seems to be the Achaeans. One of the Sea Peoples.*

Hethites: *Hebrew name for the Hittites, "sons of Heth."*

Hittites: *An Indo-European people who some centuries before 1300 BC created a literate empire in the western half of what is now Turkey. They were still powerful in the time of the early Judges, but their empire was wiped out in the invasion of the Sea Peoples and their allies. Individual Hittites had been in Canaan for centuries, probably as trader-settlers.*

Hivites: *One of the Canaanite tribes, living to the north in what is now southern Lebanon.*

Jebusites: *The Canaanite tribe that controlled Jebus, the city now known as Jerusalem. They seem to have been a mixed people, or perhaps many different peoples traded in or took refuge in Jebus in addition to the native Canaanites.*

Lukka: *Egyptian name for one of the Sea Peoples. Probably from the Lycian region in western Anatolia, the country know known as Turkey.*

Kennites: *A branch of the Midianites who had allied themselves with Israel during the time of Moses (Moses' father-in-law was a Kennite) and who, by the Times of the Judges, had become somewhat integrated into Israel.*

Midianites: A nomadic tribe or collection of tribes, probably ancestral to the Arabs, of the Sinai and western Arabia. They had been nearly exterminated by Israel under Moses, but had recovered enough to invade Israel while Moab dominated it in the time of Gideon. They had become camel-mounted raiders.

Moabites: A people living east of the Dead Sea who in the time of the early Judge Ehud had become powerful enough to dominate Canaan, thus allowing the Ammonites and Amelekites to raid the Israelites there.

Perezzites: A subgroup of Canaanites.

Phoenicians: Canaanites who lived along the coast north of the territories allotted to the tribes of Israel. Their major seaports were Tyre and Sidon. During the Times of the Judges, the people who would become Phoenicians were the Gergashites and Hivites.

Philistines, Peleset: One of the Sea Peoples, best known as the oppressors of Israel during the Times of the Judges. When the Sea Peoples were defeated in their attempt to invade Egypt, the Pharaoh turned the captured Philistines into mercenary soldiers and stationed them at not only their five city-states (Gaza, Gath, Ekron, Ashdod, and Ashnkelon) but also at such strong points as Beth Shean and Gibeah. The Philistine garrisons there were a problem to Israel. Finally subdued by King David. The Romans much later gave their name to the Land, and called it Palestine, though by then Philistia had been entirely destroyed by the Assyrians.

Plst: Egyptian spelling of word we translate as Peleset (Philistines). (Egyptian, like Hebrew, had no vowels. Their writing was entirely in consonants.)

Sea Peoples: *A mixed host of peoples who moved lock, stock and barrel around the northeast angle of the Mediterranean and flooded the east coastal area of the Sea. The first indication in the Middle East of this movement was when one component, the Sherden or Sherdan, were defeated by Rameses II in 1277 BC and its surviving men were integrated into his army. The main movement came in two waves, finally being defeated by the Egyptians about 1166 BC. So, beginning with the movement of one people, the Sea Peoples finally flooded into Palestine and drifted to a halt a hundred years later. This movement of the Sea Peoples no doubt was part of a long-simmering ferment in the area that was damped down for a while by the peace treaty between Egypt and the Hittites. The early stages of this complex of movements paralleled the invasion of Canaan by Israel. The Sea Peoples were emblematic of the turmoil of the age. To the Israelites, all Sea Peoples were "Philistines."*

Sikels, Shekelesh *(in the Egyptian language),* **Shekresh, Sikeloi:** *(in Greek) One of the Sea Peoples. They may have been from Sicily. They settled along what is now the northern coast of Israel and the southern part of Lebanon.*

Sherden: *Egyptian name for one of the Sea Peoples. They may have been from Sardinia.*

Teresh: *Egyptian name for one of the Sea Peoples. Also called* **Tursha** *(in Hittite) and* **Tyrshenoi** *(in Greek). Probably the Etruscans, a people from northern and western Italy who ruled that area before the Romans.*

Tjeker: *Egyptian name for one of the Sea Peoples. They seem to have settled at Dor on the Mediterranean coast, north of the main Philistine territory. We have no indication of where they came from.*

Tyrians: *Natives of Tyre, a commercial seafaring city on the coast of what is now Lebanon. A Canaanite people who, for some reason, avoided being conquered by the Sea Peoples and who maintained an independent city. They, together with their similarly-unconquered neighbors the* **Sidonians** *of Sidon, were later known as Phoenicians.*

www.ingramcontent.com/pod-product-compliance
Lightning Source LLC
Chambersburg PA
CBHW031859090426
42741CB00005B/565

* 9 780615 262727 *